SUMMERS IN THE BRONX

Summers in the Bronx

ATTILA THE HUN
& OTHER YANKEE STORIES

IRA BERKOW

TRIUMPH
B O O K S

For Dolly

CONTENTS

INTRODUCTION

I KNOCKED A HOLE INTO Joe DiMaggio's head when I was 10 years old, and he wasn't aware of it.

The year was 1950. I was living in a second-floor apartment with my parents on the West Side of Chicago, some 800 miles from the Bronx and Yankee Stadium and its historic playing field and distinctive rooftop façade and its pinstriped operatives. I was a Cub fan, as was almost everyone else in my neighborhood, but the Yankees had and, of course, continue to have a mystique about excellence that transcends virtually every other sports team in America. And DiMaggio was the poster boy for that team, the embodiment of the best in baseball. And so I sent away to the Yankees for a poster of—as Hemingway described him in his novel *The Old Man and the Sea*—"the great DiMaggio."

What I soon received in a manila envelope was a glossy 9 x 12 photo of the Yankee Clipper, as he was known to even us kids living on Springfield Avenue. I got myself a hammer and happily nailed the picture to my bedroom wall, driving the nail right through the *NY* on DiMaggio's baseball cap. I might have used tape, or tacked up the corners, or could have put the nail higher on the photo. But I didn't, and it was the only photo that adorned my wall.

DiMaggio was then one year away from retiring, but newspapers and magazines still carried glowing stories about this graceful man who, sportswriters said, never made a difficult catch.

I remember the picture, a rather long face, not handsome necessarily, but the face of a decent man. And I liked his eyes.

Straightforward. Believable. If, as I perceived it then, he told you you couldn't go out to play, it would be for a good reason.

Some 45 years later, when I was a sportswriter in New York and had gotten to know DiMaggio to a degree, I sat with him in the press room at Yankee Stadium before an old-timers' game, in which the gray-haired DiMaggio would, with ultimate respect, be introduced last—and also, as I learned, upon his insistence. I mentioned to him that I wanted to apologize to him.

"For what?" he asked, his eyes narrowing.

"For what I did to you in 1950."

"What was *that*?"

I told him about the photograph of him the Yankees had sent me and that I had knocked a nail through his forehead.

"You did?" he said.

"I did," I said. "But you look okay now."

He smiled. "I heal fast," he said.

Few people would place a sense of humor at the top of the list of DiMaggio's attributes, but he was quick with a one-liner in that instance. While some also found him aloof, suspicious, irritable, unapproachable, besides being a wonderful athlete, I was aware of the dark side but also had the opportunity to see yet another side of him. And in my 40-plus years as a sportswriter and columnist in New York, first for a national feature syndicate, Newspaper Enterprise Association, and then for 26 years for the *New York Times*, one of the major pursuits I had was to report on the Yankees. And in that period I reported on many of their finest players and most significant moments, as well as went back into the history of the team and the game, and shattered some myths.

In regard to DiMaggio, for example, I once asked if it was true that he never made a catch look difficult, that it was always effortless. "That's all nonsense," he said. "I remember one game I made two errors on one play. I came back to the bench, and someone asked if I wanted a war helmet to wear next inning.

"As for being a natural, well, nobody worked harder than I did. In spring training I'd have Earle Coombs, our coach, hit me ground balls in the outfield, and hit balls over my head and to my right and my left."

Or Mickey Mantle looking back on his career, with longing if not sadness. "The old days were great while they lasted," he said. "They just didn't last long enough."

Or the quirky asides that may reflect, say, the unsophistication of a rookie who, few knew, is surely destined for the Hall of Fame. I wrote in the February 22, 1993, *New York Times*, from the Yankees' spring training camp in Ft. Lauderdale, Florida: "Steve Howe was telling Mariano Rivera, a young Panamanian pitcher, about his spring trainings in high school in Clarkton, Michigan.

"'We'd go out to play in March and April and have to sweep the snow off the base paths,' the veteran relief pitcher said.

"Rivera looked at Howe, 'It snows in Michigan?' he asked."

Two seasons later Rivera joined the Yankees, at age 25, and with a sizzling cut fastball embarked on one of the most remarkable pitching careers in big-league history. He also learned firsthand as a visiting player to Detroit early in the season that indeed it snows in Michigan.

The Age of the Steinbrenner, which encapsulated most of the years that I've written sports in New York, was filled with turmoil and also numerous championships. "The Boss," as he liked being called, was smart, engaging, ambitious, and impetuous, and once told me he had "enough chinks" in his "armor to fill a battalion." And those chinks were hardly hidden. He was easy to refute, to satire, and, at times, to even admire. In other words, a joy for a columnist.

As a boy, it seemed to me the Yankees were always playing in the World Series, and often I'd develop the sniffles or some other mysterious malady to stay home from school and watch a game (the World Series in that era now so misty in history was played solely in the afternoon). One of their games against the Dodgers in 1955 was memorable to me.

Jackie Robinson, who had broken the color barrier in the major leagues just eight years earlier, doubled down the left-field line. The Yankee left fielder was Elston Howard, a black rookie. Robinson made an unusually wide turn at second, went about halfway to third, stopped, turned fully around, and stared at Howard, who had retrieved the ball. Everything seemed to stop still for a split second. Then Robinson made a motion to return to second, and the young outfielder fired the ball there to get him. Robinson arrived standing up at third.

Some 12 or 13 years later, I had an interview with the retired Robinson. Over lunch, I recalled that moment to him.

"In my imagination," I said, "I thought you were saying in effect to Howard, 'Okay, I made it, I paved the way for you, now you've got to make it on your own, and it's not easy.'"

Robinson thought for a moment, for he had a lot of World Series memories, too. "No," he said, "all I was trying to do was get an extra base."

PROLOGUE

November 5, 2009

SURE, KING KONG once held sway over the Empire State Building, but it was hardly more impressive than another monster, so to speak, who proved mighty a few miles north in the Bronx, in the sprawling new $1.5 billion Yankee Stadium. It was Godzilla wearing a baseball cap with a Yankee logo.

"Godzilla" being the nickname for the unflappable slugger Hideki Matsui, who, in the sixth and final game of the 2009 World Series, clubbed a homer, a double, and a single, driving in six runs, and, on that cool early November night, and before 52,325 roaring fans, led the Yankees to a 7–3 triumph over the Philadelphia Phillies and the franchise's 27th World Series championship.

Playing on a pair of gimpy knees—he's had arthroscopic surgery on both knees over the past two years—he was perhaps playing in his last game as a Yankee, after seven seasons with the team. He is now only a designated hitter since he is essentially a liability in the outfield, and the Yankees want to make room for younger players. Yet the 35-year-old Japanese baseball import was named Most Valuable Player in the Series, batting .615 for the six-game Series, with three homers and eight runs batted in.

"I guess you could say it's the best moment of my life," Matsui said after the game, with, typically, only the semblance of a smile.

And, sure, Matsui did not by himself win Game 6, or the World Series, or the other playoff series, against the Twins and the Angels, though he did excel in all. Game 6 might have been a microcosm of the entire season for the Yankees, with gritty Andy Pettitte, who won his first World Series game for the Yankees in 1996, winning again in this last, pitching into the sixth inning.

And a host of Yankees contributed in their way in Game 6, including and especially players who were with Pettitte on the Yankees 13 years ago—the incomparable shortstop Derek Jeter, the switch-hitting catcher Jorge Posada, and the man who closed out Game 6 and, when he comes jogging in the from the bullpen, surely appears like the Grim Reaper on the hoof to rival batsmen, Mariano Rivera.

It was Rivera, balding at age 39 (40 shortly after the Series), who entered the game in the eighth inning and shut down the final five Philadelphia batters in a row. Rivera, with a deep rocking stretch motion, his one murderous pitch, the cut fastball, still murderous, and, well, looking grim, was key again for the Yankees, who hadn't won a World Series title since 2000.

Now, nine years without a World Series championship seems an eternity for Yankee fans, most of whom were raised with the idea that entry into the World Series, if not in fact a World Series championship to boot, was a birthright.

Other fans—not to mention, but mention cries out—which include Cub fans or Pirate fans or Royal fans or Mariner fans, who hunger for a championship but are annually thwarted in their desires, find a way to live with futility. They are contented, so to speak, with the knowledge that life is, at bottom, a cruel enterprise, an odd and inscrutable business. And they learn to roll with the punches. It better suits one, the theory goes, to meet with life's inevitable and motley disasters.

Chicagoans, the fandom I'm most familiar with, having grown up in the city's limits, call their situation Realism, though others may deem it Pessimism or Fatalism or Nihilism. Shakespeare did not label it; he just illuminated it:

"As flies to wanton boys are we to the gods," he wrote. "They kill us for their sport."

But the Yankees, with the record 27 World Championships under their belt, and a record 40 league championships, seem to fortify the Gotham fans' notion that they were destined to triumph from Adam's first Evening. Or, for the team in the country's most populous city, Bigger is Best.

Maybe it was such a perception that gave vent to what in some circles became known as a great distaste for everything and anything Yankee. The legendary sports columnist Red Smith once wrote that "rooting for the Yankees was like pulling for U.S. Steel," when U.S. Steel was at the top of its game. And when humorist James Thurber said that "the majority of American males go to bed at night dreaming of striking out the Yankee batting order," it wasn't just any team that these sleeping hurlers were conquering.

But perhaps Mike Royko, the inimitable *Chicago Tribune* columnist, plumbed even deeper depths: "Actually, I don't dislike the Yankee players. Just the opposite. Many of them are approaching middle age, they're greedy and bad-tempered, they drink, get in fights, and dislike their boss. They remind me of me." And spoken by someone who admitted in print to being...a Cubs fan! And 2009 was the 101st season in which the Cubs had not won a World Series.

Like U.S. Steel, the Yankees often seemed, in their habitual winning, so cold and calculating and imperious. Yet some of the most beloved and respected ballplayers were Yankees: the Babe, Lou Gehrig, Casey Stengel ("I was told that I don't speak English too good, but I went to Europe, and they don't speak English too good over there, either"), Yogi, DiMaggio, Mantle, Catfish, Reggie, Jeter.

Now, in 2009, there was still Derek Jeter, still the prized shortstop, the clutch player, the captain who invariably does and says whatever helps the team win, including stretching himself like Spider-Man into the third row of the box seats to snare a foul ball. In the clubhouse, he is the team rock. When media attention rose to the possible controversy regarding Jose Molina replacing the regular catcher Jorge Posada in the Yankee lineup to handle A.J. Burnett (because Burnett favored pitching to Molina), Jeter said that he was sure that A.J. would do a very good job, but it would still be "kind of awkward not having Jorge in the lineup." In one fell swoop, he gave both players their props and sought to head off anything hurtful for the team's ambitions.

Alex Rodriguez joined the Yankees and famously flubbed in postseason play—seeming to psych himself with the pressure of performing with a $250 million contract over 10 years. He was roundly reviled but, following hip surgery in the spring, made a splash in 2009. He had suffered with fitting in in New York, including his publicized forays with paramours, from strippers to Madonna, and admitting taking steroids in 2003, one of his MVP seasons. I like what the TV analyst Buck Martinez told Mike Puma of the *New York Post*: "What I see in A-Rod is a genuine joy in his baseball. He went through a lot, we all know that, and he got back to being a baseball player. He reminded himself, 'This is what I always dreamed of.' And he allowed himself to be a baseball player again."

There was the ever-dependable backstop Jorge Posada and remarkable additions like the huge left-hander CC Sabathia, a whale of a pitcher, in more ways than one; and Andy Pettitte, with the profile of a cigar-store Indian, embracing important pitching assignments as he has done for the Yankees since the mid-1990s; and Mark Teixeira, in his first year as a Yankee after signing as a free agent, is the first-baseman who as a boy in Baltimore dreamed of becoming the next Don Mattingly, one of the Yankees' finest first basemen. Teixeira's improbable quest is improbably succeeding. He is a proven hitter and one of the finest fielding first basemen in baseball history, and, like another New York first baseman, the Mets' cerebral Keith Hernandez, you can almost hear the whirring of Teixeira's brain at first base as he is figuring how to outwit and out-defend the opposition. Teixeira had made a strong case for 2009 American League Most Valuable Player, leading the American League in runs batted in (122) and tied for the lead in homers (39).

In one of the several remarkable plays turned in by Yankee players in the postseason, one of the best was when Teixeira made an uncommon putout at second base. It took place in Game 3 of the American League Championship Series against the Los Angeles Angels in Anaheim. The Angels' Bobby Abreu carelessly rounded second base on a double. Yankee center fielder Melky Cabrera retrieved the ball and hit the cutoff man, Derek Jeter, who wheeled and rifled the ball to Teixeira—who had gone from his first-base position to second base!—and tagged Abreu as he tried to return to the bag.

Then the play Johnny Damon made at second base in Game 4 of the World Series was either a *Mona Lisa* in its beauty, or Keystone Kops in its madcap appearance, or both.

With a pronounced infield shift on for the pull-hitter Teixeira, Damon stole second, then popped up after his slide to find to his amazement that the Phillies' third baseman, Pedro Feliz, who had taken the throw to the first-base side of the bag, was a few feet away from him. And third base was open! To Damon, it must have looked like a water hole to a parched man in the desert. He made a wild dash for it. Feliz followed, as though chasing a man who had just lifted his wallet. Damon escaped.

But even with the best of players, something moronic can occur. Take the legitimately heralded Derek Jeter. In a key moment in Game 2 of this last World Series, he decided to bunt with two strikes on him and no outs, in order to advance the runners on first and second. Jeter is a fine bunter, but with no signal to bunt from the bench, he chose to ad-lib and bunted foul for strike three, thus possibly inhibiting a seventh-inning rally. Jeter is one of the best hitters in baseball, and here he was essentially taking the bat out of his own hands. The Yankees won the game 3–1, but Jeter admitted that he hardly helped the cause in that instance.

"Afterwards, the idea was stupid, and the execution was stupid," he said following the game, as reported by Jack Curry of the *New York Times*, "so they go hand in hand."

A good play if it works, a bonehead play if it doesn't. And it didn't. So Jeter, manfully, owned up to it.

There were other miscues by the Yankees and missed opportunities. Manager Joe Girardi, who I recall as a Yankee catcher pouncing on bunts like a glutton on a cake, making some decisions that made one raise the eyebrows. How, for example, could he put in a pinch runner for Alex Rodriguez in a late inning when the game might well go into extra innings? (Of course, he must have pressed some correct buttons over the previous eight months to bring the Yankees to the baseball pinnacle.)

Yet, from the standpoint of anyone who enjoys generally well-played baseball, it seems hard not to at least appreciate how the Yankees performed—today, as well as for nearly the last 75 years. If not even to, secretly or otherwise, even root for them—okay, if "root" doesn't rest easily in your heart or craw, then what about just "admire"?

I'm reminded of Game 6 of the 1977 World Series, the final game in which the Yankees took the Series, when Reggie Jackson hit three straight home runs against the Dodgers on three consecutive first pitches. On the last, as Jackson rounded first base, the Dodgers' first baseman, Steve Garvey, in deserved esteem, admitted after the game that he had applauded quietly into his glove.

I.

THE BOSS

A STUDENT OF ATTILA THE HUN

May 19, 1990

GEORGE STEINBRENNER WAS making a point about running the Yankees, that fifth-place enterprise in the Bronx, and about businesses in general and the people who comprise them.

"You're the leader; you're the boss," the principal owner of the Yankees was saying Thursday afternoon to a visitor in his office at the Stadium, "and you can't blame others. You must give direction.

"I've been busy recently with my shipbuilding company, I've been involved with our Olympic team, and I was named the president of the Florida Thoroughbred Breeders Association. All of that takes time. But I'm going to have to be more directly involved with the Yankees.

"I used to be very hands-on, but lately I've been more hands-off, and I plan to become more hands-on and less hands-off and hope that hands-on will be better than hands-off, the way hands-on used to be."

Many Yankee followers, however, are convinced that there has never been a hands-off period with the principal owner; it's just that when things go poorly, he leaves no fingerprints, or thinks he doesn't.

He admitted to mistakes even in his hands-on period, like calling Dave Winfield Mr. May, "which I did once, and that was regrettable"; and he let Reggie Jackson go too soon, and there was that display when he went bananas over a decision by his third-base coach in a playoff game. "But I was hot. I wanted to win. But even my mother scolded me for it. She said, 'George, I don't ever want to see what I saw you say on television.'"

He returned to the doctrine of hands-on. "You've got to be around, you've got to take an interest in the troops," he said. "Attila the Hun said it best. He said—"

"Attila the Hun?" interrupted the visitor. "The guy who pillaged and plundered?"

"Well, he wasn't perfect, but he did have some good things to say."

"Like what?"

"Here," Steinbrenner said, "I'll show you."

Seated at his desk he opened a drawer and pulled out a small book. It was *Leadership Secrets of Attila the Hun*, published last year by Warner Books.

"It's an excellent book. I've read this over and over," he said, plucking his reading glasses from his monogrammed shirt pocket. "My copy in my office in Florida is all marked up."

He flipped through the pages. "Look at this," he said, and read: "'Chieftains must inspect their Huns frequently in order to see that what is accomplished meets with what is expected.' That's what I was saying. Pretty good, huh?"

He found a red pencil on his desk, and made a check mark beside that maxim. "Here's one," he said: "'Chieftains must work hard to establish discipline and morale, then to maintain them within the tribe.'"

He read again: "'It is the custom of all Huns to hold strong to personal and national honor. This is a cardinal virtue. One's word must prevail over all other considerations, including political expediency.'"

A lot of thoughts went through a visitor's brain on that one, including the many times Steinbrenner assured a manager he was there for the season, and fired him shortly after.

"But George," said the visitor, "you don't follow all this advice."

"What I'm saying," he said, "is that we can all learn from this."

"People have said to me, 'You're like Attila the Hun,' and I get, 'You're Patton,' and, look, on every office wall I've always had that up there." He pointed to a framed document, titled "Duty as Seen by Lincoln."

But it was Attila the Hun he was quoting now, and not the Great Emancipator.

"Here's another," he said, buried in the book. "'You must recognize and accept that your greatness will be made possible through the extremes of personality, the very extremes that sometimes make for campfire satire and legendary stories.'"

He looked up over the reading glasses. "I read that one a lot," he said, with a little smile.

There was more in the book: "For Huns, conflict is a natural state." And, "Huns learn much faster when faced with adversity," and, "If it were easy to be a chieftain, everyone would be one."

"You know," he said, "I wondered if this was Attila the Hun for real, or comical. But I think it's real, or close to it."

Attila, of course, was actual, but these "Attilaisms" are simply metaphors of leadership constructed by the author, Wess Roberts, though based on historical research of that paragon of barbarity.

"'Chieftains should never misuse power,'" Steinbrenner was reading. "'Such action causes friction and leads to rebellion in the tribe or nation.' Hmm," he said, reaching for his red pencil, "I hadn't seen that one."

GEORGE AND THE
YANKEE DOGHOUSE

August 20, 1989

IN CANINE TERMS, the headline read: "Dog Bites Man." In base-ball language, it was:

"Steinbrenner Fires Manager."

No news here. News, as we know, is when Man Bites Poodle, or Retriever, or Terrier, or Springer Spaniel. Not this. The dismissal of Dallas Green—in the dismissal tradition of Lemon, Michael, Berra, Piniella, Howser, King, Virdon, and, of course, Martin, Martin, Martin, Martin, and Martin—merits maybe a line somewhere in a sports news roundup, along with, say, a darts or dominoes event.

Everybody who follows the Yankees and the singular owner understands that sooner rather than later the manager will be deposed. It doesn't matter the reason. The managers get dumped when they win, they get dumped when they lose. They get dumped when they stand up to the novel boss, they get dumped when they act like lapdogs to him. No news. Steinbrenner has exiled his managers in spring, in summer, in fall, in winter. He's fired people morning, noon, and night.

Like the perfect watchdog, teeth bared, ears cocked, he is ever ready to induce someone to hit the road, forever sniffing out an opportunity to pounce on a manager and chase him out of the park. The sign on his door might read: "Beware of Big Bad Owner."

He is to baseball what Leroy Brown is to junkyard dogs.

Some people, in trying to analyze this peculiar creature, figure him to be a publicity hound, or a mad dog, or just a big, frisky, impetuous puppy. Yankee fans and non–Yankee fans dash off letters to newspaper writers urging them not to waste ink on that arf-arf guy at the top of Yankee Stadium. "All he wants is his name in the paper," they say. "If you just ignore him, he'll go away."

Not so. If you just ignore a dog that's chewing on your cuff, it's not going to go away. It's having too much fun. And what this particular pooch does seems to have an impact on many people, all those who care about the Yankees, who love the Yankees, despite everything. "I'm a Yankee fan," a man said recently. "Even with George?" he was asked. "George doesn't play," the man replied. This is a man of iron will, a heart of unbreakable devotion, or a memory like a sieve. After all, Steinbrenner, like a beagle, has insinuated himself into the game, and no one seems able to get him off the field.

But Yankee fans persist in their pinstripe romance and want to know who the field leader is. They believe it is the public's right to know. But what difference does it make? The current helmsman, Bucky Dent, will be gone soon, anyway. Maybe next week. But old habits die hard. And it's tough to teach old dogs new tricks, etc.

And since so many people still somehow care about the Yankees, news media hounds feel it is incumbent on them to inform their readers and viewers of the change in their lives, regardless how predictable it is.

But others are reproachful. It's a comedy routine gone flat, they say. It's a song-and-dance that's old hat.

Always one wonders about the timing of Steinbrenner's moves. And serious people sit in corners and analyze the whys, wherefores, and bow-wows of the owner.

Someone said, well, attendance has fallen off, and the Yankees are 300,000 behind last year.

But the year before, they broke their single-season attendance record, and the manager, Sweet Lou, was fired anyway! The previous season attendance record for the Yankees was in 1980, and the manager, Dick Howser, was canned right after it.

Someone else wondered, well, Storm and Stress Steinbrenner wants to knock the contending Mets out of the news. But even when the Yankees were the powerhouses in New York, the owner was putting his managers in his doghouse, and then evicting them from the premises.

Some believe that Storm and Stress considers himself a master psychologist, a thinking dog's man, in other words, who conceives his moves as motivational ploys for the players.

"Doesn't he understand," said a Yankee, "that he's tried this often in the past, and it doesn't work?" In layman's terms, it means he's barking up the wrong tree.

But one thing is certain, the owner's bark is his word, his bond; you can take his bark to the bank.

For example, in the spring of this year, he said for publication: "Dallas Green will continue to manage this team this year, no matter what. I'm committed to him, and he knows it. I know that some people will say it's usually the kiss of death from me, but it isn't."

In the spring of 1982 Steinbrenner said: "Bob Lemon is going to be our manager all year. You can bet on it. I don't care if we come in last. I swear on my heart he'll be the manager all season."

Fourteen games into the season, Bob Lemon was squeezed out, and Gene Michael became the manager, followed by Clyde King. All in the same season, all within three and a half months. And by the next season a new manager, rather, an old one, Billy Martin, was back for his third of five managerial attempts.

Steinbrenner made promises of commitment to most of them, and in nearly the same language as he used for Lemon and Green.

Even the script doesn't change. So no big news.

Yet if one were to admire anything, it's the timing for this Dog Bites Man story. It is, in fact, the Dog Days of August. On second thought, with the Yankees under their Doberman pinscher owner, it always is.

GEORGE'S FIRST BLACK COACH

July 8, 1987

WHEN JOHN MCLENDON heard that George Steinbrenner had brought his name up as one of the examples that would demonstrate that there was no racism in his history, John McLendon was, he said, "amused."

The question of Steinbrenner and racism arose after the Yankee owner had used the controversial phrase "black boy" in a nationally televised interview Sunday in reference to Warren Atkinson, a black accountant for the Yankees.

Steinbrenner was on the show to discuss the problem of the hiring of members of minority groups in baseball.

McLendon was the first black head coach of a professional sports team in modern times—he coached the Cleveland Pipers of the American Basketball League, in the 1961–1962 season, or part of it.

It's been said that Steinbrenner was responsible for hiring McLendon. "In a manner of speaking, that's true," said McLendon, "even though I think he was one of the people who really didn't want me. He sort of inherited me, but I think he wanted a bigger name."

Regardless, McLendon was also the first black head coach of a professional sports team in modern times to be fired. Steinbrenner dismissed McLendon as head coach a little more than halfway through the season.

Without question, the man who fired McLendon—the first coach he ever fired—would become famous for firing people, most of whom, for the record, are white.

"After all our verbal exchanges, and my dealing with all those little tricks of his, I guess in a number of instances, if I hadn't known better, I might have thought they were racist," said McLendon. "But I knew better. We were never bitter toward each other. I knew he was a competitor, and that he was extremely ambitious about winning, though he might have been a little out of control. He didn't have losing on his mind at any time."

Steinbrenner, then 31 years old, "was a typical fan," said McLendon. "He'd holler from the stands if he wasn't happy about this play or that play."

"One time we took two vans to a game in Pittsburgh, and one of the vans broke down. I sent the key players on ahead while I stayed to fix the broken van. When I got to the game near the end of the first half, our team was ahead by 14 points. I told the team, led by Jack Adams, the captain, to keep doing what they were doing.

"At halftime, George, who came on his own, burst into the locker room. He hollered, 'Who's coaching this team, you or Adams?' I said, 'Can't you read the scoreboard? What difference does it make at this point?' Then I asked him to leave. I had told him there were two areas of the city he doesn't belong in, the bench and the locker room."

McLendon, 72 years old, now in the basketball Hall of Fame and semiretired, had been the coach of several successful black college teams, including Tennessee State, where he won three straight NAIA championships. He had also coached the Pipers of the National Industrial Basketball League, which won both the NIBL and the AAU championships in 1960. When the ABL, the first competitor in many years to the National Basketball Association, was begun, the Pipers joined it. The team had previously been owned by a group of 16 businessmen, and a 17th, Steinbrenner, whose father owned a shipping company in Cleveland, would join them.

"George didn't know who I was," said McLendon, "and it's my understanding that he and the other owners wanted someone else.

"But when the players heard that there might be a change, some told the press that they wouldn't play if I wasn't kept on."

McLendon stayed. The schedule was divided into two half seasons, and the Pipers won the first. But at one point in the second half, they lost seven of nine games. Suddenly, the players' checks were being held up, and McLendon complained. "I think that if the team hadn't been losing, we would've gotten the checks," said McLendon. For whatever the reasons, McLendon was dismissed and Bill Sharman, the former Celtic, was hired.

"I was made the director of player personnel," said McLendon. "It was the board that brought me on—George was chairman of the board—but the others I think felt that he was interfering with the team, and needed someone to deflect him a little." But racism was never a factor, said McLendon. "And when I heard the word 'black boy' used by him, I thought, 'He's a fast talker, it just tumbled out, without thinking.' George was the son of a wealthy man and always had everything he wanted. He never had to learn how to deal with people working for him. The expression he used, 'black boy,' showed an insensitivity, maybe an ignorance. It's an old phrase, but it's still a derisive term, still a sore point with a lot of people. It is with me.

"It comes out of my experience, when I was living in the South, in North Carolina and Virginia and Tennessee. It was meant to put blacks in their place, to second-class them. You go to a restaurant, and they say, 'Hey, boy, don't go in that door, go around the other way'—to a separate area. 'Black boy,' or 'Nigger boy'—not man, not adult—was the implication. In Durham once I bought some furniture, and the salesman said, 'Well, boy, sign right here, and everything will be all right.' I canceled the order.

"You listen for the terminology, to see where people are coming from. It's a kind of reference point. People who learn to communicate well avoid terms that might offend. I truly believe George wasn't being racist, he was just being George. And that's what gets him in trouble."

THE MAN WHO MISSED
STEINBRENNER

March 26, 1992

THE GOOD DOCTOR was surprised to see me. After all, it had been quite a long time since my last visit. He led me to his couch.

"A terrible thing has happened to me, Doctor," I said, lying down and propping up my feet on his furniture, "and I need help."

"Terrible?" he said. "How so?"

"I've had a certain feeling, Doctor, which has created great guilt and angst and confusion in my mind."

"Does it have anything to do with love? Marriage? Business? The gross national product?"

"No, Doctor, the fact is, I think I miss George Steinbrenner."

The doctor sprang from his chair, rushed around his office, and returned with a cold compress, which he applied to my forehead. "No, Doctor," I said, "it's not physical. It's mental."

"You're telling me?" he said, with uncustomary sarcasm.

"Doctor, I saw in the papers where George went to a baseball game the other day. Like Elvis at 7-Elevens, there had been sightings of George at ballgames, but this was the first one actually confirmed. And something stirred in me. 'Yes,' I said, 'it was right.'"

"Hmmm," said the doctor.

"And then I saw yesterday that he wrote some cockamamie letter to the other owners, saying he's tried everything he could to get back into baseball, and he wants justice, and so on and so forth.

You know there's some ploy there, some subterfuge to maybe getting a suit going even though he had a signed document that he wouldn't do it. And, Doctor, I laughed to myself when I read it."

"How loud was the laugh? A chuckle? A guffaw? Or a kind of hysteria and rolling around on the carpet?"

"Something in between. You see, I don't think I've been fooled by George in the past. I mean, I know he's often been a bully, a knee-jerk jerk, a publicity hound, a twister of facts and arms, but for all his own misjudgments and failings, I miss him. He adds something to my life."

"Your life?"

"With all the bad news every day, from the front page to the sports page, George made me laugh. He is the master of the outrageous, the king of the bizarre. He is vaudeville, Doctor. Baseball is his stage."

"You think so?"

"No, Doctor, please, no more compresses." I closed my eyes. "Yes, George Steinbrenner is vaudeville. He's a pie in the face, a kick in the pants, a pratfall on a banana peel."

"How about two fingers in the eyes?"

"That too. Listen, I wouldn't want to work for him. He berates. He screams. He makes people crazy. When you go home at night from him it's like being on a work release program. But he can also be generous, I understand, and he does a lot of charity work, especially with schools and minorities. But that's not why I miss him."

I'm not sure, because it was rather dark in the room, but I think the good doctor was now applying the compresses to his own head. I went on.

"For one thing, his teams had often been competitive. They've fallen on hard times, but that doesn't mean they won't bounce back. Even the Cubs have bounced back. Okay, let's forget the Cubs. But I think, what's so important about winning? I mean, isn't entertainment the name of the game in professional sports? And George helps entertain us. He is by far the most recognizable owner in sports. The only one close to him is Gene Autry, and who would recognize him unless he's wearing a 10-gallon hat, strumming his gee-tar, and warbling 'Tumbling Tumbleweeds'? And I'm sure that if you asked George, he'd jump up on his desk and sing for you, too. He's that kinda guy."

"Does he know 'Rudolph the Red-Nosed Reindeer'?" mumbled the doctor.

"Doctor, please, no jokes. Now, what other owner would enjoy the nickname some call him, 'Attila the Hun,' and go on to read some nutsy book titled *The Leadership Secrets of Attila the Hun*? And underline passages, and quote it to people? One of George's favorites from the book is, 'Do not expect everyone to agree with you—even if you are King.' And here's another he liked to quote: 'Chieftains must teach their Huns well that which is expected of them. Otherwise, Huns will probably do something not expected of them.'

"And what other owner has been quoted as widely as George? Remember when Goose Gossage was complaining about something? The Boss said, 'Goose should do more pitching and less quacking.'"

The doctor cleared his throat.

"Doc," I said, "will I be all right? Can I overcome this affliction of missing Steinbrenner?"

"Hmmm," he said, opening his appointments book. "Will next Thursday at 6:00 PM be convenient for you?"

THE SEINFELD *STEINBRENNER*

March 28, 1996

LOS ANGELES — Yankee fans may not always find George Steinbrenner a bundle of laughs, but a hefty slice of America does. For the last two years, a character in the guise of the Yankees' principal owner has emerged as one of the funnier aspects of *Seinfeld*, the hit sitcom.

While the real George Steinbrenner—known as "the Boss" to his minions and to tabloid headline writers—spends most of his time barking orders from various command posts around the country, the *Seinfeld* Steinbrenner can usually be found behind a big desk in his imperial office in Yankee Stadium. He always sits with his back to a camera on the set on Stage Nine in the CBS Studio Center lot here, and neither the face nor the profile of the Top Banana is ever seen by viewers.

There is only his broad back, a large, graying head, and the occasional manic flinging of arms and hands, like a man drowning. His speech pattern is arresting—a kind of tyrant staccato. As observed in a recent run-through for the show to be aired April 25, the Boss describes to an underling, George Costanza, his lunch routine.

COSTANZA:	So tomorrow, Mr. Steinbrenner, I was thinking how 'bout we try some corned beef?
STEINBRENNER:	Corned beef? Ah, it's a little fatty, don't you think?
COSTANZA:	I love it. I could have it every day.
STEINBRENNER:	No, we'll stick with the calzone.

COSTANZA: It's just that a little variety might be nice.
STEINBRENNER: Nope. I find something I like, I stick with it.
From 1973 to 1982 I ate the exact same lunch
every day: turkey chili in a bowl made out of
bread. Bread bowl, George. You'd eat the chili,
then you'd eat the bowl. Nothing more satisfying
than looking down after lunch and just seeing a
table.

Who is this Steinbrenner? It may come as no surprise to baseball
followers to learn that the *Seinfeld* version has a dual personality:
two people must play him simultaneously.

Steinbrenner, the body, doesn't speak; he merely flails. Sitting a
few feet behind him, in a slightly elevated director's chair and out
of camera range, is the prattling voice itself, contained in the slender body of Larry David, the show's 47-year-old executive producer, co-creator, writer, onetime stand-up comic, and passionate,
lifelong Yankee fan.

"I grew up in Sheepshead Bay in Brooklyn, and I've always
loved the Yankees," said David as he moved among the actors and
camera crew on the set of the show recently. "It was a kid's fantasy
that if you couldn't play center field for the Yankees—and I was a
huge Mickey Mantle fan—well, maybe you could work for them
in some capacity." And when the George Costanza character, who
is based on David and played by Jason Alexander, needed a job
after being unemployed for two years, David hit upon the Yankees.
"It's a chaotic place, and I thought George would fit in perfectly,"
he said.

So the comic possibilities were inherent there. But for David, so
is the pain. "Being a Yankees fan with Steinbrenner as the owner
is so frustrating," he said. "I was the kind of fan who even followed
the minor leaguers in the system! I knew all the players coming up.
But when Steinbrenner became the owner, they usually didn't come
up. He traded them. Nobody would make it to the team.

"And then, when he'd have good players like Rijo and Drabek
and Buhner, he'd trade them! And the free agents he'd get—the

Dave LaPoint types—were usually disasters. You just knew you could run the team better than he did."

Viewer response has been enthusiastic since Steinbrenner's first appearance on the show. The Yankees even report that George Costanza gets fan mail delivered to Yankee Stadium.

While the *Seinfeld* Steinbrenner may be impetuous, irascible, and despotic, he can also be generous and warmhearted in his impetuous, irascible, and despotic style.

The voice was inspired by Steinbrenner himself. "I don't know the man," David said, "but from seeing him interviewed on television and seeing his quotes in newspaper stories, I came up with this version of the way he speaks, the going on and on, on subjects, and going from one topic to another almost without stopping for a breath."

Jerry Seinfeld, leaning against the couch in his apartment on the set, said, "Larry wanted to get an actor to say the lines on the show, but when I heard his interpretation, I said, 'This is great. It's funny. You read the lines.'" And the guy who plays him now? "Excellent. He has a very gifted back of the head. I guess all that is needed to play George Steinbrenner is the back half."

Seinfeld and David had called Steinbrenner to ask permission to use his name and the Yankees for their show. "At first he was confused," Seinfeld said. "He thought that the George character played by Jason was supposed to be him. I told him, no, that we'd had that character in the show for five years. But he gave us the permission, and I think it's a credit to him. A lot of people take themselves so seriously that they have refused to allow us to portray them on the show."

One of the show's writers, Jeff Schaffer, said that the Steinbrenner character is Every Boss. "He can fire you on a whim," he said. "And this one is the Renaissance man of mindless things."

Another writer, Alec Berg, said, "Actually, the less we know about Steinbrenner the better. We can do or say just about anything to caricature him."

What does Steinbrenner's body have to say for itself? And, by the way, whose body is it?

When the head of Steinbrenner the Body turns around, the broad face of one Lee Baer, an actor, is revealed.

And where did he come from?

"From central casting," Baer said. Of course. Where else would you expect George Steinbrenner to come from?

"I got a call that they were looking for a Steinbrenner looka-like," Baer said. "I don't know anything about George Steinbrenner other than that he owned the Yankees. I don't follow baseball. I don't really follow sports. I like old cars."

Baer is a large man, 59, and there the relative similarity with the Boss ends.

He speaks with all the animation one expects from an under-taker, not the perfervid Steinbrenner. "I used to do a little stand-up comedy," he said. "Deadpan. Dry humor."

Actually, Baer is a relatively new Steinbrenner. Another extra had done it, and when he couldn't make it for a show, Baer was brought in.

"We liked his mannerisms, like the crazy way of pointing in the air," David said, giving a loony impersonation, "and decided to keep him."

But it is David who delivers such Steinbrenner lines as the one to George Costanza when he shows up after being presumed dead and finds out he didn't get the promotion he expected. "Well, once you were dead," Steinbrenner says, "we couldn't just sit on our hands. We had to move."

Or when Costanza tries to get his secretary a raise and tells Steinbrenner that she supports an entire family, including a sick mother, and that she can't afford to go out to lunch so she goes to a nearby school cafeteria and pretends to be a teacher. Steinbrenner commiserates. "You know," he says as he reaches for a ringing phone, "she'd be better off making a sandwich and bringing it in."

On a show last December, Steinbrenner said, "Sure, I like a cup-cake every now and then, like everybody else. You know, I like it when they have a little cream on the inside. It's a surprise. That's good. Plus the chocolate ones are good, too. Sometimes I just can't even make up my mind. A lot of times I'll mix the two together, make a vanilla fudge…"

Speaking by telephone from his office in the Yankees' spring training complex in Tampa, Florida, the real George Michael Steinbrenner III said, "Sweets are one of my weaknesses—I can't deny it. I like chocolate, I like doughnuts. My favorite doughnuts are the glazed from Krispy Kreme. I'm a freak for glazed doughnuts. And I like the jelly ones from Dunkin' Donuts, too. People around here know I like them, and when I make a talk or an appearance at some place, someone usually brings over a box of a dozen doughnuts for me."

Steinbrenner said he had seen only a couple of *Seinfeld* shows. "They're very good, very funny, very well written," he said. "It's amazing how popular the show is. And my grandchildren love it. My oldest is nine years old, and he thinks being on that show is the greatest thing I've ever accomplished in my life. The writers are terrific. I'm impressed with the detail, even down to the names in the Yankees' parking lot. I was prepared not to like the show, but I came away laughing my head off.

"Hey, if you can't laugh at yourself, you're in bad shape," he continued. "We need more laughs today. I go to too many funerals and not enough birthday parties.

"And, yes, I've come to be called the Boss. Nobody loves the Boss, especially a hard-nosed Boss. I am a tough boss, no question about it, but I don't demand anything from the people who work for me that I don't demand from myself. Maybe that comes across on the show, too.

"My favorite episode on the show? That was the funeral scene where I go to the home of a grieving family, and the father sees me and he's hardly concerned that his son is no longer with us. He hollers at me, 'How could you trade Buhner?'"

Steinbrenner laughed. "It was sick," he said, "but hilarious."

II.

THE CRACK
OF THE BAT

SO MANY HITS,
SO MUCH TIME FOR JETER

August 30, 1999

IT WAS A BEAUTIFUL, butterscotch day. Yankee Stadium was bathed in sunlight, and Derek Jeter, who seems to move in perpetual sunshine, was at bat. Jeter cocked his bat in his customary stance, the bat held in such a high, unorthodox manner that it appears he is sprouting an antenna from his helmet. It was the third inning, runners on first and third, none out, and the Yankees were behind 2–0 to Seattle pitcher Paul Abbott. Abbott, a right-hander, threw, and Jeter, a right-handed hitter, whipped the bat around with the speed of a mongoose attacking a lizard, and lined a single to right field, the 762nd base hit of his major league career.

The myriad statistics that baseball elicits can give one a headache, but a particular number that Jeter is fashioning is remarkable. It places him in a category with the greatest hitters in baseball history. With his two singles yesterday in the Yankees' 11–5 victory over the Mariners, he has more hits in the first four full years of his career, 751 (he had 12 in 1995), than hitters like Ted Williams (749 in his first four seasons), Cal Ripken (745), Lou Gehrig (736), Ty Cobb (729), Pete Rose (723), and Henry Aaron (718) had. If Jeter continues at his present, league-leading pace of hits (175)—he is batting .348, third in the American League to Nomar Garciaparra's .350 and Bernie Williams' .349—Jeter projects to 220 hits this season and 796 hits for his first four full years. He will have passed Stan Musial (792) and Joe DiMaggio (791).

"If," said Jeter, seated at his locker before yesterday's game, "man, *if*'s a big word. Baseball's a game of failure. Obviously, you fail more than you succeed."

His track record as well as his persona portray anything but the concept of failure. At age 25, he appears the most level-headed of athletes. He is approachable and, as Yankee management has learned, coachable. "He's not one of these young guys who thinks he's got it all figured out," the Yankee coach Jose Cardenal said.

In the other clubhouse, Jamie Moyer, a Seattle pitcher, said Jeter had made "huge adjustments at the plate."

"When he first came up," said Moyer, "it was obvious he had talent, but he also had some glaring holes. For one thing, you could pitch him up and in, get him out on his front foot—that is, get him to shift onto his front foot before he swung. You did that with change of speed, and it took a lot of sting out of his bat."

But, added Moyer, Jeter adapted. "That hole no longer exists."

It doesn't exist because Jeter spends good chunks of his time at his craft. While his reputation of dating stars like Mariah Carey may be earned, it has not proved a debilitating distraction to his occupational chores.

Over last winter, he regularly appeared on the Yankees' Tampa spring-training grounds to work on driving inside pitches to left field, instead of fighting them off and slicing them to right. He didn't find this kind of diligence extraordinary. "I live in Tampa," he said, with a shrug. "I work on my game all the time."

Don Zimmer, the Yankees' dugout coach, who has been in professional baseball for 51 years, said that unlike some superb hitters, like Pete Rose and Wade Boggs, Jeter hits with power, and to all fields. "How do you think he hits balls over the right-field fence— tapping them?" Zimmer said. "He's got a big swing, and for him to have so many hits is phenomenal."

Jeter is also a good-size shortstop, at 6'3", 195 pounds, bigger and with greater range and richer than Johnny Pesky, whom Zimmer remembers as having a terrific major league start. Pesky was a Red Sox shortstop in the 1940s and had 779 hits in his first four seasons. Pesky got 208 hits in his second season with Boston, in 1946, and batted .335. He dropped slightly in 1947, getting 207 hits with a .324 batting average.

"But they made him take a cut in pay after that season," Zimmer said. "He was a coach for me when I managed the Red Sox, and Johnny told me he's never forgotten that he went from something like $7,000 a year to $6,000."

Jeter, to underscore a difference in eras, went from $750,000 in his third year to $5 million this year, after arbitration. But he says there are no hard feelings about that between him and George Steinbrenner, the team's principal owner. "But he gets upset when Michigan beats Ohio State in football," said Jeter, who is from Michigan while Steinbrenner is from Ohio, "and I do get on him about that."

Jeter, who grew up a Yankee fan in Kalamazoo, said that his favorite player was Dave Winfield, who was not one of Steinbrenner's favorites. "I thought Winfield was the greatest all-around athlete there was," Jeter said. And as far as Winfield's being Mr. May, as Steinbrenner had disparaged him, Jeter said, "He must have got a lot of hits in May then, to get 3,000 for his career."

As for his career numbers, Jeter said: "I just want to be consistent and play as long as I'm having fun. I hope to have a lot of great years left. After all, I'm still the youngest guy on this team."

Looking around the clubhouse of the defending World Series–champion Yankees, it turned out he was right. Only 25. Just a babe. Which gives rise to yet another agreeable, if plump, historical baseball image.

WHEW! SCOOTER TALKS CIRCLES AROUND THE HALL

August 1, 1994

COOPERSTOWN, NEW YORK — Somewhere in his acceptance speech into the Baseball Hall of Fame yesterday on a hot day behind a school beside a cornfield, like something out of *Field of Dreams*, and with who knows how many thousands of people because a lot were sitting, many were standing, and many others lolled on the hilly grass, somewhere in that speech Phil Rizzuto, speaking without notes and without what sometimes seemed a semblance of rhyme or reason—not that anybody in the loving, laughing audience seemed to care, least of all the Scooter himself, who in his inimitable and wondrous digressions and ramblings actually began with "Holy cow!" since it took him 38 years after the end of his baseball career in 1956 to finally make the Hall of Fame.

Anyway, somewhere in the speech he told about leaving home in Brooklyn for the first time when he was 19 years old and going to play shortstop in the minor league town of Bassett, Virginia, and he was on a train with no sleeper and when he got his first taste of southern fried chicken and it was great and it was also the first time that he ever ate—"Hey, White, what's that stuff that looks like oatmeal?"—and Bill White, his onetime announcing partner on Yankee broadcasts, and, like all his partners, never seemed to learn their first names, though he knew the first and last names of a lot of the birthdays he forever is announcing and the owners of his favorite restaurants even though as he admits he seldom talks about the score or the game, but after 38 years of announcing games and after a 13-year playing career with championship Yankee teams few seem to care about this either, well, White was in the audience and stood up and said, "Grits."

"Grits!" announced Rizzuto. "That's right. And I didn't know what to do with 'em so I stuffed it in my pocket."

There isn't enough space here to get into Rizzuto's whole recitation of being raised in Brooklyn and his family that means so much to him, especially his wife, Cora, and his baseball career or his time in the Navy during World War II when he even got seasick on the ferry from New Jersey to Virginia and people said, "He's going to protect us?" and how he said he starts stories at the end and goes back to the beginning and winds up in the middle but he paid tribute to many, including two he was inducted into the Hall of Fame with, Leo Durocher and Steve Carlton, and told a story of Durocher being a great bench jockey as well as a great manager and when he popped a ball straight up and the catcher caught it in a World Series against the Dodgers, Durocher hollered, "That's a home run in an elevator shaft!"

And Carlton, sitting right behind him on the dais with some 30 Hall of Famers, threw back his head and laughed, old Stone Face and old Mum Mouth to the reporters, even though they voted him into the hall on the first ballot and he did thank them for it, but Lefty to the ballplayers who loved him if he was their teammate and hated him if they had to face his wicked slider and fadeaway fastball said that everything seems to come in cycles.

It was at Cooperstown in an exhibition game during induction week in 1966 that Carlton was called up to the St. Louis Cardinals after having been sent down to the minors to pitch on that day to the Minnesota Twins and he struck out 10 batters in 7 innings and went on from there to strike out more batters than anyone in baseball history outside of Nolan Ryan and also performed the amazing feat in 1972 of winning 27 games for the Philadelphia Phillies, a forlorn, last-place team that won just 59 games altogether that season and also said another old Phillie, Richie Ashburn, should be in the Hall of Fame. And should.

But—where were we?—oh, yes, Carlton said that he didn't talk to the news media because he needed to focus on pitching and couldn't be distracted, something Rizzuto never minded, and after about 20 minutes of his 30-minute confabulation, Rizzuto said that if his voice held up—it was getting hoarse and he was also embarked on combat with a few flies at the podium—that he could talk for a long time and if anybody wanted to leave they could and Yogi Berra and Johnny Bench, laughing like everyone else, got up and started to walk out and Rizzuto explained, "They took so many balls in the mask."

Someone in the crowd asked whose birthday it was and Rizzuto, looking natty in his blue blazer and silver hair, mentioned Ruby Sabattino, "who is getting along in age," he said, "and was a little under the weather and couldn't make it up to Cooperstown and, oh, the cannolis, the cannolis came last night—a day without cannolis is like a day without sunshine!"

And then he said that this was the last part and he had written something down and adjusted his glasses and said he can't read it and doesn't want to start crying, though he knows it's okay in a situation like this—just before him was the actress Laraine Day accepting for her late husband Durocher, often a bad actor on the ballfield, and beside her their son, Chris, who broke down when he said it was unfortunate that his dad couldn't be here for this honor but felt "my father stands here with us because he got time off today for good behavior."

Rizzuto was able to read now, gravel-voiced and emotional, and said, "I had the most wonderful lifetime any man can possibly have. And I thank you for this wonderful game they call baseball."

And everyone understood this perfectly, and laughed between tears, or cried between laughter, or just stood and cheered. Baseball was never better.

MANTLE AND HERSCHKOPF
THE PSYCHIATRIST

July 23, 1989

MICKEY MANTLE OFFERED his head to Herschkopf the Psychiatrist for inspection. It happened like this:

Last week, in the restaurant in Manhattan that bears his name, Mantle, the former slugger and Hall of Famer, was the host for a brunch for some of the retired players who had participated in the Yankees' Old-Timers' Game. It was around noon, and Mantle had been sitting at a table in the back section with Billy Martin. Martin was wearing sunglasses because, presumably, noon on Sunday is still very early.

Mantle looked only a little wan himself, but chipper, in black sweater and slacks and a red shirt open at the collar. He rose and walked over to greet a sportswriter. Mantle, now 57, and retired as an active player for 21 years, retains a boyish look. His hair is still blond though streaked with gray, and his blocky body, at 5′11″, still looks as if he could turn on a fastball and drive it out of the park, for homer number 537. Mantle and the writer shook hands. "Mickey," said the writer, "I'd like you to meet a friend, Dr. Herschkopf. He's a psychiatrist."

Mantle, instead of extending his hand to Herschkopf the Psychiatrist, extended his head. Go to work, Doc, the gesture said.

It brought a good laugh, even from the bearded psychiatrist. After all, it is widely known that psychiatrists are never allowed to laugh. But an exception could be made, since the only photograph of a ballplayer that Herschkopf ever taped to his wall as a boy in Washington Heights was a picture of Mickey Mantle.

Now, before Herschkopf the Psychiatrist could accept the offer and spring into action to probe the noodle of Mantle, a man with a camera interrupted: Could he take a picture with Mickey?

The old star agreed, and the man asked a bystander to take the picture. Just as the bystander was about to press the button, Mantle interrupted, "It generally works better when you take the lens cap off."

He laughed. Soon more people showed up for an autograph, and more. Suddenly Mantle was besieged. They converged around the sportswriter's table. "Sorry I'm doing this to you," said Mantle. He wasn't laughing, and whispered something to Bill Liederman, who runs the restaurant. Mantle signed a shirt, a ball, a book. Once, he was asked to sign a dinner roll from the breadbasket, and did.

Now a fan asked him to sign a bat. Mantle asked, "Who should I make it out to?" "Just your name is fine," the man said. Mantle said to Liederman. "I'm tellin' you, they're collectors. That's it!" And Mantle turned and left.

A Louisville Slugger bat costs about $10, but one with Mantle's actual signature can be resold for $250. If it is personalized—that is, "To Elmer, from Mickey Mantle"—then it has little value. So there is a good business going on. Mantle is aware of how it works, said Liederman, and doesn't like to be exploited.

"Also," said Liederman, "his knees are so bad from all the operations in his playing days that it hurts for him to stand for long. Usually he's very patient with autographs when he's sitting."

Herschkopf the Psychiatrist observed all this. "You know," the sportswriter said, "Mantle used to talk about a recurring dream after he retired. In the dream, he tries desperately to get into a ballpark during a game, but all the gates are closed."

"It's funny," said Herschkopf, nodding without smiling. "People don't realize how revealing dreams can be. I think the manifest content of this one reflects how inadequate, how left out, he felt, that without baseball he was lost."

The writer said, "I remember talking to Mantle in 1972, when he was 40, four years after he had retired, and he told me, 'Playing baseball is all I've ever known. It makes me kind of bitter that it's all over. You look around and see other guys my age who are just starting to reach their peak in other jobs. And I'm finished. I wouldn't trade my baseball career. But I'll tell ya, I'd give anything right now to be a lawyer or something.'"

For years Mantle had also expressed a fear of dying young because there had been early deaths in his family, including his father, who died at 40.

The sportswriter recalled Mantle on a cold December evening in 1985 in a hotel suite in Fargo, North Dakota. Mantle was there with other mourners for Roger Maris' funeral—Maris had died of cancer at age 51—and he was comforting Maris' widow and childhood sweetheart, Pat. She sat on a sofa, and Mantle, pale, in stocking feet, knelt in front of her and held her hands in his.

One imagined Mantle thinking not only of Maris' mortality, but of his own as well, and how unaccountable it was that his former teammate's life had been taken before his.

Through the years, Mantle has attempted numerous businesses, and many failed. The restaurant in Manhattan, however, appears to be doing well. And Mantle spends many of his days playing golf with clients and others who pay to be in his presence, attending banquets and card shows, and in general earning a living as a celebrity.

"Sometimes," said Liederman, "the thing Mickey wants more than anything else is just to be left alone."

"I always thought that the cross Mantle had to bear was that he could never again be Mickey Mantle," said Herschkopf the Psychiatrist. "But now I realize that the cross he has to bear is that he can never stop being Mickey Mantle."

A FINAL, SWEET OVATION
FOR MANTLE

August 26, 1996

THE SUN WAS HIGH in the sky, the white clouds were pillowed against the light-blue universe, the No. 4 elevated train rumbled somewhere in the distance, and the fans at Yankee Stadium were nestling into the furniture. It was a beautiful day for a ballgame and for a sentimental journey. Yesterday the fans had both.

In a ceremony before a cheering crowd of 50,808 that not only preceded but temporarily upstaged the Yankees' pursuit of a third straight victory against Oakland and Andy Pettitte's attempt for his 19th victory of the season, a monument in honor of Mickey Mantle was unveiled in an area behind the left-center-field fence.

"This is great day for us," said David Mantle, one of Mantle's three surviving sons, "and a sad one, too."

Mickey Mantle, who died on August 13, 1995, at age 63 from liver cancer, was, like the other three Yankees with a monument, a posthumous recipient.

In the nearly century-old history of the Yankees, only four men have been honored with monuments in Monument Park, although many plaques for Yankee stalwarts, as well as two for visiting Popes, have been hung out there. Miller Huggins, the manager of the legendary Yankee teams of the 1920s, was the first to be monumentalized, as it were. The next was Lou Gehrig, and, 47 years ago, the third was for Babe Ruth.

The ceremony yesterday included Whitey Ford, Mantle's good friend and longtime teammate in the 1950s and 1960s, unveiling the monument, which was already in place. Ford happily was not asked to carry the slab of granite in, since it weighs 4,500 pounds.

Joe DiMaggio, among several of Mantle's former teammates as well as Mantle family members, was on hand, looking as dapper as ever, though, at age 81, gray-haired, rheumy-eyed, and slightly stooped. It was mentioned to him earlier in the day that George Steinbrenner, a certain Yankee administrator, had said that DiMaggio could have a monument out there any time he decided to have it. DiMaggio smiled wanly at the thought. "I'd rather it not be now," he said. "I'm too busy living."

And while the monument would contain the mammoth Mantle statistics, such as 536 home runs in his 18-year career, most World Series homers (18), three-time Most Valuable Player award winner, Hank Bauer would remember something else.

"I think of that interview he gave on television near the end of his life," said Bauer, a former teammate of Mantle's, "when he said to the kids of the country, 'Don't put me as your hero. I'm not a hero.' What he was sayin' was, if I had known I could have played longer, I would have taken better care of myself. I played with him, and I thought that that was outstanding."

Ford said, "He felt he made a bad example of himself with his drinking and carrying on for 40 years." But like many, Ford remembered another side of Mantle, one that was warm, gracious, and funny. Ford recalled that Mantle, who played center field when the monuments were actually in play near the fence there, used to say, "Whenever Whitey pitched, I'd always have to be circlin' those monuments."

Billy Crystal acted as a stand-in for the legion of Mantle fans, an inspired choice because he was genuine, and because he is good. "Toward the end of Mickey's life," he said, "a new person emerged." Mantle had undergone a liver transplant and in the short life left to him became a strong advocate for organ donors, now reaching past a relatively self-absorbed, sybaritic life into one of greater awareness and humanity. Crystal had come to know

Mantle and believed that Mantle then "came to grips with himself. It was perhaps his finest hour."

The outpouring of affection for Mantle from the literally tens of thousands of cards and letters and good-luck amulets seemed to astonish Mantle. He never realized the effect his baseball life had had on so many people. For in imagination he remained the country boy with flaxen hair from Commerce, Oklahoma, the all-America-seeming lad, the guy who, as in the storybooks, hit a ton, ran like the wind, and then suffered crippling leg injuries that rendered him sometimes gimpy. As an announcer on a giant-screen replay of Mantle in action said yesterday, the way he played in pain "enhanced his heroic stature, because in the end it made him appear vulnerable, like you, like me."

And this is the Mantle that Crystal remembers when, as a boy living on Long Island, he was taken by his father to his first big-league game, on May 30, 1956, and saw Mantle, a switch-hitter batting left-handed, hit a long home run against the right-field façade. "And I became a Mickey Mantle fan," he said. "I was nine years old and I limped for no reason. I gave my bar mitzvah speech in an Oklahoma drawl."

Crystal concluded that "in my mind's eye, and in all our minds' eyes" Mantle "will always be playing."

Soppy, but with substance. Thus the reality relating to such striking performers as Mantle in such dream-invoking activities as baseball.

And then the current Yankees took the field against the A's. It seemed vaguely anticlimactic.

DIMAGGIO, A NEIGHBOR,
THE QUAKE

October 24, 1989

SAN FRANCISCO — Joe DiMaggio is her neighbor. She has lived for about 10 years just a few doors down the block from the old Yankee ballplayer in the Marina District here, the lovely, snug area that took so terrible a jolt from last week's earthquake.

"I'd see Mr. DiMaggio in the grocery store, or just walking down the street, but I never spoke to him," said Sherra Cox. "He's a quiet man, seems like a nice man, but I never felt right just walking up and talking to him, or getting his autograph. I suppose it's okay for kids to do."

Cox, a middle-aged woman, smiled with some difficulty because of the stitches under her lip. She sat Sunday afternoon in a chair beside her bed in San Francisco General Hospital. Above her on a small television screen was the 49ers-Patriots football game. She's a sports fan. A week ago today, she hurried home to her second-floor apartment from her job as manager in an accounting firm to watch the third game of the World Series. Suddenly, at 5:04 PM, the earth shook violently, the floor she stood on opened like a trapdoor, and she tumbled down, the rest of the building crashing around her.

She lay trapped under a door and doorjamb for some time. How long she doesn't know. She smelled fire, felt the creaking of the

35

wood and stone around her, and thought she might be burned or crushed to death. She told herself, "Don't panic." She prayed.

A firefighter named Jerry Shannon would crawl in and spend the next two and a half hours struggling to dig her out.

"He was so reassuring," Cox recalled. "He said, 'Don't worry, when this is over I'll buy you a cup of coffee.'"

Shannon went through two chain saws, used two jacks to prop up the wood around Cox, and finally resorted to a hatchet. He thought they might not make it, but told himself not to think about it, just to "stay busy."

When Shannon discovered her, he told Cox he had to get equipment. "Don't leave me; I don't want to die in here," she pleaded. He promised to return.

"You're my hero," she told him later, on the stretcher, in the night lighted by flames, and she kissed him.

Now, a visitor said he'd seen in the newspaper a picture of her neighbor, DiMaggio, a 74-year-old man in sports jacket and open-collared shirt, waiting in a long line at a shelter with other neighbors to learn whether his house would have to be demolished. He'd been at the ballgame the night of the quake and escaped injury. Three doors down from his two-story home—and directly across the street from Sherra Cox's—three people perished. DiMaggio's house suffered some damage, but was saved.

Curious, said the visitor, that one of America's most celebrated men, one who has been raised to hero status, now elderly and white-haired, was in the end, like everyone else, simply trying to survive. Meanwhile, all around, courageous acts by unsung firefighters, rescue workers, and everyday citizens were being performed in the aftermath of the earthquake.

"I wonder what the definition of hero is?" Cox said. "I suppose it has to do with saving lives."

There are people like Jerry Shannon, and those who crawled through the wreckage to find bodies in cars flattened to the size of license plates, who will never do a television commercial or be pictured on a bubble-gum card. This is no knock at those upon whom we confer the title of model or hero. It says more about the values of a nation that so prizes entertainers, including ballplayers, even those as fine and decent and elegant as Joe DiMaggio.

"I've thought for a long time," Rick Reuschel, the Giants' pitcher, said the other day, "that ballplayers are elevated way too high. And when a disaster like this happens, we see how unimportant our job is in comparison to so many others."

Sherra Cox, meanwhile, feels that the Series should continue in the Bay Area.

"Life goes on," she said. "We pick up the pieces. And I'm rooting for the Giants!" The visitor had brought something for her. He had been to the rubble and debris that was once Cox's home and noticed a book among the shards. He picked it up—the only book he saw—just before a bulldozer could scoop it up. The book, with a purple dust jacket, was a little torn and charred but in otherwise good shape. He handed it to Sherra Cox.

"I had that book," she said. "I had hundreds of books, and records, and I bought that one but I hadn't got around to reading it."

Reflectively, she ran her fingers over the title. The book is by Truman Capote. It is called *Answered Prayers*.

"My goodness," Sherra Cox said. Her eyes were moist. "I think I'll have to read it now."

DIMAGGIO, FAILING, IS 84 TODAY

November 25, 1998

IN THE PRESS ROOM of Yankee Stadium not long ago I saw Joe DiMaggio sitting at a table with a few friends. Even in repose he looked elegant, still trim in his dark suit, hair graying and thin but neatly coiffed. I was reminded of a remark by Henry Kissinger when he sat near DiMaggio in the owner's box in Yankee Stadium. The Yankees had lost a playoff game, and Kissinger, on the way out, had said, "Joe, put on a uniform—they can use you." In the mind's eye, Joe still could lope after a fly ball....

Today, which marks DiMaggio's 84th birthday, one wonders if he can heal as he lies in a hospital in Hollywood, Florida, amid reports that he has been battling lung cancer as well as pneumonia. He is fighting for his life. One wonders whether the man who once hit in 56 straight big-league games, a record that has stood for 57 years, can summon the energy and, perhaps, the requisite miracle to regain health.

Even before his admission to the hospital on October 12, DiMaggio's name was in the news, in an indirect fashion. The Yankees' sterling center fielder, Bernie Williams, the American League's leading hitter and Gold Glove fly-chaser, heir to DiMaggio and Mickey Mantle, and a free agent, has been in controversial negotiations with the Yankees. Williams is as distinguished a ballplayer, if not as iconic, as his famous predecessors.

It is difficult for fans to imagine that their athletic heroes are vulnerable to everything human. The youth of the ballplayer, or, sometimes, even the coach, is eternal, if only in photographs and film—DiMaggio in his baggy pinstripes is still rapping out hits in his familiar long stride and sweeping stroke of the bat—and in our memory.

Red Holzman can still be seen in that fashion in the huddle, instructing Bradley and Frazier, and Weeb Ewbank may be forever visualized discussing strategy with a mud-splattered Joe Namath on the sideline. In that sense, Coach Holzman of the Knicks and Coach Ewbank of the Jets, who died recently, remain vital to us.

And Catfish Hunter, because of the Lou Gehrig's disease he has, may soon lose such control in his muscles that he will be unable to even grip a baseball. Such thoughts seem to fall off the radar screen of our comprehension.

And so it is with Joe D., that intensely proud man, that sometimes impatient and unforgiving man, who, the Yankee management knew, would be insulted if, at Old-Timers' Day, he should not be the last announced.

In the press dining room before one of those old-timers' games, I gave DiMaggio a photograph of him and Marilyn Monroe taken by Richard Sanborn, who is now a judicial magistrate living in Maryland. Sanborn had been a sergeant in the Army stationed in Tokyo in 1954 when DiMaggio and Monroe went on their honeymoon to Japan. I had done a column on DiMaggio, and Sanborn sent it to me to give to DiMaggio, saying he had always wanted Joe to have it and didn't know how to get it to him. Would I do it? I did.

As most people know, bringing up his former wife to DiMaggio would end any conversation with him. It was too personal. But I handed DiMaggio the photograph. He thought it was great. "And this guy was just an amateur photographer?" DiMaggio said. "I've got to send him a note and thank him."

Shortly after, alone with DiMaggio, I said, "Marilyn looked beautiful in the picture." "She was beautiful," DiMaggio said, as though relating an insight.

I said, "Joe, there's a question I've always wanted to ask you, if you don't mind." He nodded, knitting his brow. "There's that great anecdote first written by Gay Talese," I went on, "about when you were in Japan and Marilyn was asked by the brass to entertain the troops in Korea. When she returned to your hotel room, you asked how it went, and she said, 'Oh, Joe, you never heard such cheering!' And you said quietly, 'Yes, I have.'

"Did it happen?"

"Yes," DiMaggio said, "it did."

ROGER MARIS COMES HOME

December 20, 1985

FARGO, NORTH DAKOTA — The townspeople and visitors from around the area and those from far away filled the pews, while others stood quietly against the wall of St. Mary's Cathedral here at noon yesterday.

More continued to enter the century-old red brick church, brushing the snow from the shoulders of their coats and stamping their feet to bring circulation back, having braved the snow and a temperature of 2 degrees above zero to be here. There were about 900 in the main church and another 100 or so in the basement, where they sat on folding chairs and watched the funeral mass on closed-circuit television. ("This is the most people we've had here," said a priest in a maroon robe, "since the bishop died a year ago November.") People entering the church were handed a program. On the back was a photograph not of a renowned cleric, this time, but of a baseball player in a pinstriped uniform. He was in full extension while swinging a bat. It was a portrait of youthful power—the man was then 27 years old.

The man's jaw was tight with purpose, and so were his considerable muscles. The picture was taken on October 1, 1961, in Yankee Stadium, on the last day of the season. It was a historic day in sports—and, in many ways, in the social fabric of this country.

That swing, on that day, resulted in the 61st home run of the season for Roger Maris, breaking the revered, 34-year-old, single-season home-run record held by Babe Ruth.

It has been said, and is probably so, that it was the most dramatic assault on a sports record ever. Much of the nation followed closely Maris' pursuit of the ghost of Ruth.

The man who hit that home run was in the coffin covered by a white sheet in front of the altar.

Roger Eugene Maris died Saturday after a long bout with lymphatic cancer. He was 51 years old. Fargo was where he had grown up, though he had made his home in later years in Gainesville, Florida. "He requested that he be buried here," his wife, Pat, had said. "His roots were here. These people were his people."

It was here that he met Pat when both were high-school students, and it was here that on the night of the senior prom he rang the bell of her home and shyly handed her a corsage.

It was here that as a halfback for Shanley High he once led his team to a 33–27 victory over Devils Lake by running back four kickoffs for touchdowns. "It got so," the Devils Lake coach had said, "that we hated to score."

It was here in Fargo that Maris began his professional baseball career, with Fargo-Moorhead of the Northern League in 1953, right out of high school, and where he hit .325 and nine homers.

It was from here that he went, eventually, to play in the summer sun for the Indians, the A's, the Yankees, and the Cardinals in a 12-year career, hitting 275 home runs, knocking in 851 runs, and batting .260.

Here, in a shopping mall called West Acres, there is the Roger Maris Museum. It is a 74-foot-long, glass-enclosed case with many significant baseballs and bats from his career, and pictures from grade-school basketball to posing when a Yankee with President John Kennedy.

It was in front of that museum that three wreaths had recently been laid.

And it was in Fargo and the rest of the state that Governor George Sinner proclaimed that on this day all the state flags in North Dakota be lowered to half-staff in honor of a favorite son.

In St. Mary's now, near the coffin, were Maris' immediate family: Pat, and their six children—four boys and two girls—ranging in age from 28 to 20. Close by were Maris' mother, Corinne, and his father, Rudy, a retired railroad man but still with the strong hands of someone who hammered ties for the Great Northern.

Across the aisle, in dark suits, sat some of Maris' Yankee teammates and baseball friends, retired now but still with the strong hands of men who could throw a baseball swiftly and hit it far. They were among the pallbearers. There was Whitey Ford and Moose Skowron and Clete Boyer and Mike Shannon and Bob Allison and Whitey Herzog and Mickey Mantle. Mantle, his blond hair graying, held a white handkerchief and wiped his eyes and nose.

Bobby Richardson, the Yankee second baseman and teammate of Maris, delivered the eulogy, talking about Maris the person and Maris the ballplayer. He recalled a time when Maris, the old right fielder, visited him. They went to see one of Richardson's sons in an American Legion game. The lad, playing right field, misjudged a fly ball and turned it into a hit. Maris poked Richardson and said, "He's been watching me too much."

Maris, in fact, was an excellent fielder. But to some, the notion that Maris had a sense of humor at all might seem strange. He often had a miserable time with the press, especially from that 1961 season on when he suddenly emerged as a candidate to break Ruth's record.

There were some old-timers who resented the assault on their idol, including apparently the then-commissioner of baseball, Ford Frick, who considered putting the now infamous asterisk alongside Maris' name in the record book—for Maris had played a 162-game schedule, while Ruth's was 154 games.

The heat on Maris was terrific, even greater off the field than on. "Reporters were all over him every day down the stretch," recalled John Blanchard, the former Yankee catcher who had come to Fargo. "One day I saw his hair was falling out of his crew cut. I said, 'Roger, what's wrong? You got the heebie-jeebies or something?' He said, 'Nerves, but the doctor said the hair would grow back.' That's how tense it became."

Maris appeared sullen at times. "But he was misunderstood," said Richardson. "He was a private man who wanted to go home after the game, be with his family. He didn't take much to the acclaim and adulation of the hero."

Maris was a direct man from the northern plains, and these were his people, he felt. The screaming masses were not whom he lived for. When his uniform, No. 9, was retired by the Yankees last summer, he made a special mention on the field of friends who had traveled from North Dakota and who were sitting behind the screen.

Now some of those friends were packed into the church. And they, along with the family and the old ballplayers, soon left St. Mary's. Under a white sky and across the now-white barley and wheat and sugarbeet fields, they drove in the funeral procession to the Holy Cross Cemetery in North Fargo.

And it was there, with snow falling on the pine trees and the breath of people steamy in the frigid air, that Roger Maris was buried.

REGGIE: OLD "44" RETURNS

April 28, 1982

AT 3:30 YESTERDAY afternoon, under the threatening sky, Reggie Jackson came out of the visitors' dugout at Yankee Stadium to take batting practice. He was carrying his familiar black bat and wearing his familiar mustache, but the uniform was not the customary one.

It was the red and white of the California Angels and not the blue pinstripe of the Yanks. This was his first time back to New York City in a baseball uniform of any kind since the World Series last year.

Now it was a full four and a half hours before the start of the ballgame. Earlier in the day, at a news conference for a baseball shoe he is sponsoring, Jackson said he was feeling "skittish" about returning to New York. "I've got butterflies," he said.

The end of a turbulent and dramatic five-year career with the Yankees came over the winter when the owner of the team, George Steinbrenner, a shipbuilder by profession, did not renew his contract.

The stands were empty now, and the loudest sound was the rumble of the Woodlawn elevated train just beyond the park. There were no cries of "Reg-gie, Reg-gie," as there had been for the last five years in which he was a Yankee. The chant had continued this season as well whenever the Yankees fell behind. The fans hoped that Steinbrenner the Shipbuilder would hear their displeasure over the loss of the slugger.

And there was no one now floating through the stands wearing a Yankee cap and a white bedsheet with No. 44 on the back. Stepping into the batting cage now was no ghost, this was the real thing—or what has been passing for the real thing.

Reggie, after all, was hitting only .173 this season, with no extra base hits—he had nine singles—and only four runs batted in—and three of those RBI coming when he made outs.

"I had heard about the chants and the guy dressed like a ghost," Reggie had said. "I'm just glad they don't read the stats." Jackson hit for 40 minutes off Coach Bobby Knoop, sometimes lunging at pitches and sending them up to stick in the screen of the batting cage, and sometimes, with that powerful, rippling stroke, driving balls crashing deep into the blue right-field seats.

After the batting practice, Jackson was brought into a room for another news conference. He was affable, even mellow. "I guess it's a matter of maturity, of getting older," he said. He will be 36 on May 18. Jackson has had difficult personal experiences with the Yankees, from battles with Billy Martin, the former Yankee manager, to Steinbrenner the Shipbuilder. And now he is trying to do well with a new team and struggling.

"I've been not wanting to come back and then wanting to come back," he said. "New York City is still the place I'm very familiar with, still like very much. And the people have been great, warm and receptive."

He was asked what's wrong at the plate. "I'm just not feeling comfortable at the plate, in my home turf—and I don't know why." Was he trying too hard? "That's part of it, I'm sure. I'm trying to hit three home runs at one time at bat." Are you sorry about leaving New York? "I would have loved to finish my career here. But George didn't think it was the thing to do." Jackson had become a free agent after the 1981 season. Was he ever made an offer by the Yankees? "No." He went on: "I was kind of made a fool of. George cast doubts about whether I could play anymore, about my worth and quality and character to be a Yankee.

"I got tired of being run down by him." Reggie's voice softened. "I didn't want to prostitute myself to come back, I wasn't going to bow down to the guy." Now the Angels were about to take official batting practice. And when Jackson came down the runway to the dugout, he stepped on white towels—the old white-carpet treatment—set out by Rod Carew. Carew introduced him to the assemblage of photographers.

Jackson laughed, fooled around at the bat rack for several minutes, then stepped out onto the field. The small early crowd cheered as they saw Reggie's number: 44 on the scoreboard, the digital clock read 6:44.

When Jackson ran out to play right field in the bottom of the first inning, the crowd of 35,458, most holding colorful umbrellas against the thin rain, gave him a standing ovation and the familiar Reg-gie chant. Later, a guy in a T-shirt would run out and present Jackson with a bouquet of yellow flowers.

In the second inning, batting in the sixth position against Ron Guidry, he popped up very high to second base. He was clearly trying to drive the ball out of the park, and he was clearly disappointed.

In the fifth, Jackson singled past second base. It was a good shot, but it wasn't what he wanted.

By the seventh, the rain was coming down harder. Jackson would be leading off. Manager Mauch was out talking to the umpires, trying to get the game called since the Angels were ahead 2–1.

But the game continued. Jackson toweled off his black bat, wiped his glasses, and stepped into the batter's box. On Guidry's first pitch, he swung. The crack of the bat resounded through the park. The ball rocketed. Jackson dropped his bat, clapped his hands in pure and unadulterated delight. The ball was into the right-field upper deck for a home run before he had taken three steps.

There was a moment of shock, then the fans thundered applause. And chanted his name, and kept chanting it so that, after he had ducked into the dugout, he was forced to come out into the rain and wave his arms to them.

When Jackson departed into the dugout, shortly another chant began, starting slowly, and then swelling until the entire ballpark was throbbing with it. It was an obscenity directed at Steinbrenner, who was in the ballpark—and repeated over and over. It was chilling.

After the inning, Jackson was replaced in right field by Juan Beniquez. For Jackson, though, the game was complete. And on this rainy, miserable April night, the home run was a moment to remember—his first extra-base hit of the season.

REGGIE BECOMES
MR. COOPERSTOWN

August 2, 1993

COOPERSTOWN, NEW YORK — On a hot August afternoon, Mr. October rose to the occasion, again. Center stage, as we had come to expect of him, all alone, and in front of a huge crowd of some 10,000 people, Reggie Jackson became the 216th member to be inducted into the Baseball Hall of Fame.

Shouts of "Reg-gie! Reg-gie!" rang out from fans on a sprawling meadow. And the man in the dark suit, white shirt, aqua tie, and broad shoulders standing under the canopy acknowledged the familiar chant with an empyrean nod, befitting this moment of ascendance into baseball's Olympus.

He came armed with a speech filled with emotions, with memories, with personal moments, with viewpoints about the state of the game and with a sense of appreciation and even gratitude for what he was, as well as who he became. It was a home run. A rather long home run, about 30 minutes in length, but isn't that what we had come to expect from Reggie, too?

Among the 38 Hall of Famers who returned to Cooperstown for the event was Catfish Hunter, a teammate of Jackson's with both the Oakland A's and the Yankees. Hunter preceded Jackson to the Yankees. "Reggie hit the clubhouse talking," said Hunter, "and guys on the team asked me, 'How come nobody killed this guy in Oakland?' I said, 'Just listen to him for two minutes and then walk away. He'll still be saying the same thing an hour later. But it doesn't matter. He'll help you win.' At the end of the year they said, 'Cat, you were right.'"

George Steinbrenner, who courted Jackson as a free agent and signed him to a $2.96 million contract for five years in 1977, was in attendance. "I think it's appropriate that Reggie is alone as an inductee," said Steinbrenner. "Fits his personality." Steinbrenner said that Jackson was "the definition of a star."

But Jackson unexpectedly defused what in times past resembled an ego as great as any of the towering blasts he cracked.

"You remember a player with the Yankees named Mickey Rivers?" asked Jackson. "Well, he said I had a white man's first name, Reginald; a Spanish middle name, Martinez; and a black man's last name. 'And that's why you're so fouled up.'"

And when he introduced his father, Martinez Jackson, a former tailor who is 90 years old and lives in Philadelphia, he asked him to stand. His father did and waved to the crowd. "Dad," he said, "no more applause. You're stealing my thunder."

It was his father, he said, who was his greatest influence, who taught him pride in being a black man, even though his father lived in a time when he was considered a second-class citizen, but who instilled in his son the dream of "climbing the ladder of equality."

And it was his father who reminded him that he had to speak correctly, to form his words so that they would fit his thoughts. "And no un-unh, no nope, no yep," said Jackson.

Reggie, though, would grow up in a different generation from Martinez Jackson, when he could be anyone he felt he wanted to be. And of the athletes of his time, Reggie said that Muhammad Ali, who was making his presence known in the early 1960s while Jackson was a college student at Arizona State, was a guiding light. Ali talked, regardless of the perceived effect on the listener. Jackson listened and learned. "He gave me the confidence to speak out and to be proud of who I am," said Jackson.

While Jackson wasn't in a league as a figure in racial matters as Ali had been, or, another of the models that Jackson referred to yesterday, Jackie Robinson, he took personal stands against what he saw as unfair treatment by a manager—Billy Martin, particularly—

or Steinbrenner. And he saw himself in historical perspective. As he said, "I'm a real fan," and he remembered the struggles of black predecessors, including those in the Negro Leagues. "It was a time when they knocked at the door," he said, "but nobody let them in."

While he played for the A's, Orioles, Angels, and Yankees, it is as a Yankee that he enters the Hall of Fame, a bronzed Yankee cap resting on his bronzed image on his Hall plaque. And while there may have been some deal between Steinbrenner and Jackson for a job as a consultant to the Yankees' principal owner, for the greater glory of both, Jackson still talks most movingly about his experience as a Yankee. "When you play in New York, everything is intensified 1,000 times. And the fans there play a special role. I'll never forget you. You're the best."

Earlier, Hunter had recalled when the fans once pelted Jackson with his Reggie! candy bars, which shot briefly across the chocolate firmament. But, after a homer or two, they were again eating out of Reggie's hands.

Jackson took a look at the game today and was concerned. "The humanity of the game" cannot be lost. "The game of Williams and Mantle and DiMaggio and Clemente" should not be overcome "by the economics."

Returning to himself, he said, "I know I wasn't the best—just look behind me, and I know that"—seated behind him on the podium were folks like Musial and Spahn and Feller and Frank Robinson. "But when the roll is called, sooner or later they've got to call my name."

As Mickey Rivers might have noticed, Reginald Martinez Jackson, the man with a profusion, if not a confusion, of names, had got it right.

BLOMBERG:
ONE AWESTRUCK ROOKIE

March 14, 1969

FT. LAUDERDALE, FLORIDA — The click of cleats on the cement floor, the palaver of the players and the reflexive pounding of fists into leather mitts: the sounds of a baseball locker room were silent now. Only a few New York Yankees remained. Ron Blomberg would be the last to leave; he is savoring every moment.

"I just sit here on the bench," he said, in front of his stall, "and stare at the names on the lockers. Joe Pepitone, Whitey Ford, Rocky Colavito. Oh, gosh, and Mickey Mantle, No. 7. Whew."

The Yankees exhibition game against Baltimore had been called because of rain. Now Blomberg, after doing wind-sprints in the drizzle, had showered and was wearing a white turtleneck shirt, brown slacks, short brown hair with bangs Caesar-style, and a bright, wide look in his light brown eyes.

Blomberg, a 20-year-old outfielder, was the top draft choice in the major leagues in 1967. He signed with the Yankees when he walked off the stage after graduation from an Atlanta High School. ("I can't say what the figure was," he said, "but newspapers had it anywhere from $35,000 to $150,000. Name a figure, and they wrote it.")

"My biggest disappointment is not seeing Mickey Mantle play," he said. "He was in the locker room earlier today, to pick up some things. I had never been this close to him, and I watched him from here and I whispered to myself, 'Is that really you, Mickey?'

"I went over and shook hands with him. Oh, boy. He's not that tall, but I'll tell you, that's some kind of build. His arms are so big and, oh, his legs, so powerful.

"Later on, he crumpled a piece of paper and tossed it near here. Where is it? I got it someplace," said Blomberg, rummaging through the spiked shoes and boxes of Milk Duds and Bazooka bubble gum in his locker. "I can't find it right now. But I wanted it for a souvenir."

Blomberg, after his second professional season (he batted .251 with seven homers for Kinston of the Class A Carolina League in 1968—"My worst year ever. But I learned a lot"), was invited to the Yankee training camp here. He expects to be farmed out again soon, this time to a Triple A club.

"Right now, it's like I'm in one world, and all around me is another world," he said. "In a year or two, maybe I'll be part of that other world, too. Can you imagine, me at Yankee Stadium? If I'd ever hit a home run I'd just stand on first base. I wouldn't know what to do, I'd be so excited."

Lindy McDaniel, the graying relief pitcher, walked by.

"Those were three great innings you pitched yesterday," said Blomberg.

"Do my best," said McDaniel, pleasantly.

"You will," said Blomberg, sort of stuck for words.

"That's Lindy McDaniel," whispered Blomberg to a newspaperman, when McDaniel was out of earshot. "He's a great pitcher."

"It feels so funny, being here. If the president were here and asked me over for tea, well, that's the way it's like.

"But I want to make it for good. And I really think I didn't care about that bonus money. I just wanted to play baseball. When I was going bad at Kinston, I'd stay up until 4:00 in the morning swinging a bat in front of a mirror, getting blisters like crazy.

"The other day I played my first major league game, two innings against the Senators. I didn't bat, but I was thrilled just to play. In front of Ted Williams, too. I felt like running over for his autograph.

"Look over there. That's Mantle's uniform, No. 7. Whew-weeee. I'm No. 29. I hope some day that people look at my uniform number that way. It's a little dream. No, it's a big dream. Say, it's like I'm a dreamy guy, huh?"

O'NEILL MOVES ON GRACEFULLY

November 7, 2001

THE TALL MAN with the familiar gentle face, his eight-year-old son at his side, entered Yankee Stadium for the last time yesterday morning as a member of the Yankees. He happened to glance ahead, and through the tunnel he noticed a piecemeal view of the park. *How bright the green grass looked in the sunshine,* he thought, *how beautiful.*

He allowed himself now a pang of nostalgia—not regret, but a sweet remembrance of things past, of the excitement of games and pennant races that never paled for him. He had rarely taken notice of this sight through all these years when hurrying from the players' entrance to the locker room, but on this day, this bittersweet ending, he paused.

Paul O'Neill had come back to the Stadium to pack up the contents of his locker. He will not be back. After 21 years as a professional baseball player, 17 years in the majors, the last nine as a Yankee, the man many consider—pardon the platitude—the heart and soul of championship teams (five World Series appearances with the Yankees) and championship attitudes, as well as right fielder exemplar and left-handed clutch hitter in the middle of the lineup, is retiring, at age 38.

"Feels strange," he said, in sweatshirt and jeans, as, with a little help from his son Aaron he placed items into a large cardboard box that will be sent to his home in Cincinnati. "I've never cleaned out my locker before. I mean, everything. And I didn't work out today.

Usually, right after the last game, you go back to working out, preparing for next season."

Paul O'Neill, who led the Yankees with a .333 batting average in this Series, remained in many ways the symbol of the Yankees who, whether they liked it or not, whether it truly applied or not, came to symbolize for multitudes the grit of the city as it attempted to pull itself up from of the unspeakable attack on September 11.

They had come from behind to win games in stunning fashion. Then they lost the last game of the season, the postseason, in stunning fashion. The team had flown back from Phoenix after the less-than-agreeable conclusion of the World Series Sunday night. Would he come back for an old-timers' game?

"The way I ran to third Sunday," he said, "I already did." This was a joke about his having been thrown out at third in the first inning after hitting a ball into the right-center-field gap. What he didn't say was, Arizona had to make a perfect relay to get him, but he still set a tone for aggressive and intelligent play.

Baseball, though, wasn't as pleasurable as it once was for O'Neill because, he said, "this hurts, that hurts." "I wasn't as productive as I once was," he said. So O'Neill had decided before this season that this would be his last, but didn't emphasize it because, typically, he didn't want the attention.

But playing baseball games could still be thrilling. "When I first came up to the majors, in September of '85, with Cincinnati," he said, "I wondered how guys like Rose and Concepcion and Perez could be so cool about playing, while I was shaking in my boots. But, you know, I always got butterflies before games, my whole career, and was happy I did. The adrenaline was always there, the excitement was always there."

He said he had been dubious about coming to New York, in 1993, when traded from Cincinnati. "I came here not knowing what street the Empire State Building was on, and I became a part of the community, and it was where my three children were born," he said. "It was the best nine or 10 years of my life."

Like most Yankees, he was uncomfortable with having the team looked at as a symbol in these tragic times. "If we gave joy to people, and helped in a small way to unify the city, that's wonderful," he said. "But for me, there are two different stories—there was life and death, and there were baseball games."

His future? Spend time with his family, maybe do some baseball broadcasting. Few, however, will forget the warm, appreciative chants of "Paul-ie, Paul-ie," that rose from the 56,000 fans crammed into Yankee Stadium in his last home game, Game 5 of the World Series, last Thursday night. It is guessed that rightly his number, 21, will be retired by the Yankees.

As for the Yankees in this Series, "Sure, it was disappointing to lose, especially with a close game in Game 7," he said, "but it was Arizona's time. We did all we could. Don't think anyone could do anything more."

Which mirrors precisely what Paul O'Neill has done and meant for the Yankees, their fans, and the City of New York.

MURCER: YANKS' LAST LINK
TO BYGONE DAYS

June 23, 1983

BOBBY MURCER, who as of last Monday no longer plays for the Yankees, was recently talking about his singing career. "A guy I know came to me one day last winter when I was home in Oklahoma City and asked if I could sing," said Murcer. "I said, 'Why, you must be crazy. Of course I can sing.' But I was kidding. I had never sung before, except in the shower. No, once I did it to a pack of dogs. They seemed to like it. It was my only true test in front of a crowd.

"But the next day this guy comes back and says he's written a song. He's a lawyer by trade, but he has written songs. He said he wanted me to sing this song. I said, 'I can't sing.' He said, 'You told me you could sing.' I said, 'I was lyin'.'

"So he tells me he's booked a studio and gone to other expenses and says I can't let him down. Well, I went and cut the record." The name of the song was "Skoal Dippin' Man"—Murcer is a ruminator of Skoal, a chewing tobacco. And what happens? Some listeners—not canines this time—heard it and liked it, and Murcer and his friend sold the song to Columbia Records.

It was released last month, and it's now selling well and playing on radio all over the country—including the country-music station that broadcasts the Mets' games. WHN was a little slow in playing it. "Well, yes," Joel Raab, program director of the station, said yesterday. "We had to be sure it was a hit because he's a Yankee."

Was. Was a Yankee. After a 17-year career in Major League Baseball, nearly 13 of them with the Yankees—he also played with the Giants and Cubs—Murcer was cut from the roster, at age 37. The move was not a surprise to Murcer, but the finality of it still came as a shock. Yet he took it with the grace and good humor that Yankee fans have come to associate with Bobby Murcer. And although he is now in the music business, there is no need for weeping violins.

Sitting not long ago in front of his locker at Yankee Stadium, rocking in his rocking chair, he was asked when he might play next. A schedule was on the wall nearby. "Let's see," he said looking up, "this is May, right? Hmmm, Oakland comes to town in the last week in August."

He could joke without bitterness, but he was never happy about playing infrequently. "Am I embarrassed? Yes," he'd say, "at $400,000 per year." He was convinced, though, that he could still play. "In baseball, when you get into your thirties they just assume you can't do it anymore." But it seemed whenever he was sent up to pinch-hit, or on those rare occasions to play as a designated hitter, he'd often come through.

One of the most moving was August 6, 1979, when the Yankees returned from the funeral of Thurman Munson, their catcher, who had been killed while flying his private plane. The team flew in from Canton, Ohio, and had to play the Orioles at the Stadium that night. Murcer, a close friend of Munson's, had delivered one of the eulogies at the funeral. He wasn't going to play, and then asked to be in the lineup. He drove in all the Yankee runs with a three-run homer in the seventh and a two-run single in the ninth, as they came from behind to win 5–4.

"I never used that bat again," said Murcer. "I sent it to Diana." Diana is Munson's widow. The last home run of Murcer's career came three weeks ago, on June 1, against the Angels. He started as the DH, and in the sixth inning cracked a pitch into the right-field seats to make the score 1–0. It was the deciding hit, and the Yanks won 3–0.

That was only his 12th at-bat of the season, and the crowd of 28,427 gave him a standing ovation. They kept cheering while the next hitter, Ken Griffey, was at the plate. "The fans wanted me to take a bow, but I didn't want to disturb Ken," said Murcer. Griffey grounded out, but the fans still cheered Murcer. So then several Yankee players and Billy Martin, the manager, urged him to go out so they could get on with the game.

"I tipped my hat and waved," said Murcer. "It made me feel good. The fans have always been kind to me. I guess a lot of it was just remembering me as the last link of bygone days."

Those were the days of the mid-1960s, of Mantle and Maris and Ford and Berra, players who, of course, are still fondly recalled by Yankee fans.

For the last few years now, it seemed that Murcer was always on his last legs as a Yankee, the legs that first appeared at Yankee Stadium in 1965, at shortstop, when he was 19 years old. "And with straw in my hair," he said, "I was that green."

Coming out of Oklahoma and playing shortstop before being moved to center field and being blond and talented, he was, it seemed, a carbon copy of Mickey Mantle. Even to being signed by the same scout, Tom Greenwade.

Beyond Mantle, he seemed heir to the Yankee legacy extending back to Ruth and Gehrig and DiMaggio. Unlike those fellows, it seems certain that Murcer will never be bronzed in the Baseball Hall of Fame. But Murcer was good. Though not big—at 5′11″ and 180 pounds—he could hit with power. And he could run and throw and chase a fly ball with elan across the turf. He had a .277 career batting average with 252 homers.

Then last Monday morning, he received a phone call from George Steinbrenner, the principal owner of the Yankees. The two had spoken on several occasions about the possibilities of Murcer's being cut from the roster. It seemed that every time it was imminent, Murcer did something noteworthy—like get 10 straight hits last spring training—to "buy some time," as he phrased it.

"George and I have a special relationship," said Murcer, who accepted a job as a Yankee announcer from Steinbrenner. "I've known him ever since he took over the Yankees in 1973. He told me that they were going to make a roster change, and that I could take a job in the broadcasting booth, which I wanted, if I wasn't going to play.

"He said he just didn't like seeing me settin' in the corner of the dugout. He was very gentle about it, very concerned. If I had raised a stink he might not have done it. I really think so. I know I can still hit, and I think I can still help the ballclub. But I said, 'I want to do what's best for the team, George.'

"I can't say I loved it, but I knew that one day this day would have to come. It happens to everyone."

MATTINGLY'S ELUSIVE DREAM

July 29, 1994

HE WAS A 16-YEAR-OLD high school kid in Evansville, Indiana, when he saw Reggie Jackson on television wallop three towering home runs in one game for the Yankees in the 1977 World Series against the Dodgers. That's when he first pictured himself in a World Series, for the Yankees. A World Series he might be close to now, but a World Series that might elude him again if there is a baseball strike.

"It got me excited when I saw Reggie do that, really pumped me up," Don Mattingly said yesterday in front of his locker at Yankee Stadium before the Red Sox game, his eyes bright with memory. "I'd always been a Reds fan because we lived relatively close to Cincinnati, but that's when I first started thinking Yankees."

He sat in a green baseball cap with the logo of a construction company, black polo shirt, jeans, and bare feet, the toes wiggling slightly in the Yankee-blue carpet. Even now, at age 33, and with neatly trimmed black mustache, one still could envision the high school kid, pumped up.

He joined the Yankees in 1982, the year after their last World Series appearance and, in his 11-year career, has become one of the best players in club history. Unlike most of his renowned predecessors, however, from Ruth to DiMaggio to Mantle—whose pinstriped spirits remain palpable from their monuments in center field—he has never had the chance to play in a postseason game of any sort.

At his locker, at about 10:45 AM, he waited for word from the players' union about a strike date, which seemed inevitable, since the owners the day before had rejected the players' union's counterproposals.

"I still dream about playing in a World Series," he said. "I picture myself making the great play—of diving for a ball, getting a big hit with men on base, wanting to know how I'd react under that kind of pressure and if I could take my game to another level, like Paul Molitor did in last year's Series. But where I am now, and how I got here, is more important than me being in a World Series. I have to look at the big picture, not just at the small picture, which is me."

Mattingly, whose salary is $3.62 million this season, understands this: "I'm in a fortunate position, all of us here are, and I know that we've got here because of the guys before us who fought for our rights."

But even as late as a few years ago, when he was the player representative for the Yankees, he was not as committed as he might have been.

"I met Curt Flood last year at a banquet in the off-season," said Mattingly. "And we talked about how he stood up to the owners, to seek free agency. He was blackballed, as I understand, but he opened the door for McNally and Messersmith to sue baseball for free agency." His toes dug into the carpet.

Other older players, like Mickey Mantle, had filled him in on more history. "Mickey was saying that he'd hit 50 home runs, and they'd cut his salary 10 percent. Told him he didn't have as good a year as the year before."

The players' union, he said, has done a good job of keeping the players abreast of negotiations, as well as informing them of their history. Of how the owners want to put a cap on the free market, in essence, by putting a cap on salary. Of how the owners want to take back, for example, salary arbitration, for which the players had fought so hard in the last 20 years.

Today's players also learn that when free agency and salary arbitration were instituted, baseball had a gross revenue of $50 million. Gross revenue last year in baseball was $2 billion, with salaries rising only proportionately. Mattingly has talked with Steve Howe, the Yankees closer, who was a rookie with the Dodgers in the last big strike in 1981. Howe told him, "The owners were crying poverty then, too. Same story, same script."

Mattingly also understands that the owners, as in the past, have been reluctant to show their operating books, but when they have, the players have seen how a team may, for example, have owner-ship in common with another company and make non-baseball charges to the ballclub. This practice is not illegal, but it hardly makes the owners' case that they should change the free-market system as they have it.

As for possibly sitting home in October and missing the World Series because of a strike, he said, "I think I'm like most of the play-ers, if it has to be, it has to be. I don't want that to sound cold. But we couldn't wait to make our stand after the season. We'd have no leverage then. We have no choice but to act now."

He soon got the word: the players will strike August 12 if there is no agreement with the owners. He accepted it soberly. Mattingly was now in uniform and wearing his baseball shoes, and no longer the barefoot boy. A lad's fantasy had given way to a man's reality.

WINFIELD:
ONE DEFINITION OF A WINNER

March 19, 1983

IN BETWEEN RUNNING a baseball team and operating a shipbuilding company, George M. Steinbrenner III has also found time in his busy schedule to assist lexicographers.

He recently was of invaluable assistance to them in adding to the definition of the noun *winner*. In Webster's New Collegiate, *winner* is defined as, "One that wins; a: one that is successful esp. through praiseworthy ability and hard work b: a victor esp. in games and sports."

Steinbrenner generously has added to this: "c: one who wears a World Series ring. That is, a member of a team that has won the World Series." The definition may have come to him in a dream, or perhaps it was arrived at after long hours at a desk while wetting meditatively the tip of a pencil. No one is quite certain. The ways of the wondrous are strange, indeed.

Steinbrenner referred specifically to one of the laborers on his baseball team, Dave Winfield, an outfielder. "Until you wear one of these," Steinbrenner had said, pointing to a ring he wears from the 1977 Yankees' world championship, "you are not a winner. Winfield is almost there."

Winfield, upon hearing this a few days later, said about Steinbrenner, "He bought a team that won. Hey, the clubhouse guy's got a ring. The ticket guy's got a ring. Think about it."

Winfield is in his third season as a Yankee, after playing the first eight years of his career with a poor club, the San Diego Padres. In Winfield's first season with the Yankees, he helped them get into the World Series, in which they were defeated by the Dodgers.

Last year, the Yankees did not make the World Series. But Winfield had a very fine season. He led the Yankees in most offensive categories, batting .280, with 106 runs batted in, 37 homers (third in the American League), and a slugging percentage of .560 (second in the league). His 17 assists were tops among the league's outfielders, and he won a Gold Glove for fielding excellence.

But Winfield has yet to be on a team that has won the World Series.

Forget his individual achievements, forget that a team consists of 25 players. By Steinbrenner's definition, Dave Winfield is a loser. So is Ty Cobb. So is Ted Williams. So are Nap Lajoie, George Sisler, Harry Heilmann, Paul and Lloyd Waner, Gabby Hartnett, Wee Willie Keeler, Sam Crawford, Early Wynn, Luke Appling, Joe Cronin, Hack Wilson, Babe Herman, Chuck Klein, Ted Lyons, Robin Roberts, and Ernie Banks, among others—each a member of the Hall of Fame and each of whom never played on a team that won the World Series, though some played in the Series.

The boob Cobb could do no better than a record .367 batting average with a record 4,191 hits over a 24-year major league career. The wretched Williams, the last man to hit .400—.406 in 1941—could only muster a .344 career mark and 521 homers. Cobb was on three pennant winners, and Williams one. Neither ever a winner. But talk about losers, Ernie Banks never was on a team that even got into a World Series! You wonder how he ever played 19 years and hit 512 home runs and was twice named Most Valuable Player in the National League.

Now there are many players who have won World Series championship rings, and some of them, of course, are in the Hall of Fame, as well. But some aren't.

George William Zeber wears a World Series ring; in fact, from the same team that Steinbrenner wears his. Perhaps not many remember Zeber. He was an occasional infielder on the 1977 Yankees, and on the 1978 Yankees, which also won the Series. But he played in only the '77 Series, against the Dodgers, pinch hitting twice and striking out both times.

His career totals are: 28 games, 71 times at bat, a .296 batting average, 3 doubles, 0 triples, 3 home runs, 10 runs batted in, 0 stolen bases. In contrast, Winfield's career record is: 1,362 games, 4,924 times at bat, 735 runs, 1,399 hits, 228 doubles, 48 triples, 204 home runs, 800 runs batted in, and 149 stolen bases.

But, as defined by Steinbrenner, Winfield is a loser and Zeber a winner.

Some people confuse George William Zeber with William Henry Zuber, another winner. Zuber was a pitcher for the Yankee team that beat the Cardinals in the 1943 World Series. Zuber didn't get into a single game, but Zuber, like Zeber, got a ring.

And like Zeber, Zuber would get into one World Series game when, with the 1946 Red Sox, he pitched two innings and gave up three hits, one walk, and one run.

There was also Rollie "Bunions" Zeider. But in contrast to Zeber and Zuber, Zeider was a loser. In the 1918 World Series, he was a replacement at third base in the late innings of two games for the Cubs, who lost in six to the Red Sox.

The next time the Red Sox were in the World Series was 1946— it was the team of Ted Williams and William Zuber—and they lost to the Cardinals. One of the winners on St. Louis was a catcher named Clyde Kluttz, who did not get into even one of the seven games. But he got his ring. It is a curious point of history in that 31 years later, Mickey Klutts, an infielder with the Yankees, would emerge as a winner. Like Kluttz, Klutts didn't get into a game, either. But Kluttz and Klutts, like Steinbrenner, all wear World Series rings without ever having appeared in a World Series box score.

Steinbrenner also has a ring from the 1978 Series, as do performers named Brian Doyle, Gary Thomasson, Ken Clay, Fred Stanley, Cliff Johnson, and Mike Heath. All except Steinbrenner and the clubhouse guy and the ticket guy played in that Series.

Meanwhile, Dave Winfield is in spring training with the Yankees to try once again to earn a World Series ring and finally become a winner, a winner, that is, as defined by George Steinbrenner, the owner of a team that last season finished in fifth place.

WIGGINS TOUCHED THE HOT IRON

January 15, 1991

JACK MCKEON could hardly believe his eyes, or his luck. It was the first time he saw Alan Wiggins, in 1980, when McKeon, the new general manager for the San Diego Padres, was scouting his Class A Reno club.

"We were playing at Lodi," said McKeon, "and this tall, slender kid who I had never heard of leads off the game for Lodi, singles, steals second, steals third, and scores on an infield out. The next time up, he does the same thing. I'm thinking, *Wow, this kid's got some kind of charisma.*"

Wiggins belonged to the Dodger organization, but McKeon was able to draft him over the winter. "I had to take a chance on this kid," said McKeon. "And the following season he was in the big leagues."

McKeon had recalled this after learning that Wiggins, who had been in the major leagues for seven seasons but had been out of baseball for the last three years, was dead, at the age of 32.

An obituary on January 9 read: "Alan Wiggins, a once promising major league baseball player who undermined his career with drugs, died at Cedars-Sinai Medical Center in Los Angeles Sunday night." Cause of death was announced as pneumonia and other complications, including tuberculosis. But there remained speculation. Wiggins, who had played at 160 pounds, weighed less than 70 pounds when he died.

And yesterday the *Los Angeles Times* reported that doctors and one family member and some friends said Wiggins had AIDS; an official in baseball familiar with Wiggins' condition confirmed the player was suffering from the disease.

"I saw Wiggy just before I went to spring training last season," said Tony Gwynn, "and he looked like he hadn't had a meal in three days." Gwynn was Wiggins' closest friend when they were with San Diego and had batted behind him in that wonderful season of 1984 when Wiggins stole 70 bases, still a club record, batted .258, and ranged far at second base to help the Padres win the National League pennant. He then batted .364 in the World Series loss to the Detroit Tigers. He would sign a four-year contract for nearly $3 million. "He was our catalyst," Gwynn said.

Now Wiggins—who had come so far from a childhood in Watts he had described as "hard"—had fame, fortune, a wife and child (he and Angie would have three children), and a bright, bright future. Oh, what a dream.

"He started coughing, and we put him in the hospital," said his mother-in-law, Anna Wood, recently. "He went down so fast."

In July 1982, in Wiggins' first full season in the major leagues, he was arrested for possession of cocaine and underwent drug treatment. In 1985 he appeared on television spots urging youngsters to stay off drugs. Then, just a few weeks into the season, Wiggins fell into drug use again and returned to rehabilitation. Upon his release, he was traded to the Orioles.

"It took a while for me to understand that it is a disease," said Wiggins of his drug problem. "It's something that you have no control over. It's a battle that you will have to fight for the rest of your life."

With the Orioles, he still seemed moody—"He was always kind of low-key and introverted," said McKeon—and sometimes quite distant even from his teammates. His agent, Tony Attanasio, said that much of it had to do with Wiggins' intelligence. "He actually read books and the front page of the newspapers," Attanasio said. "Some players resented it."

In June 1987 Wiggins was in New York and, with a few Yankees and Orioles, agreed to speak at two junior high schools as part of

Mayor Koch's drug prevention program. Wiggins wore a light blue suit and salmon-colored tie and looked as though the subject was difficult for him. He stood straight and spoke softly. He said that unfortunately some people don't learn from their mistakes, but that he had. Wiggins told this story about his baby boy: "I warned him that he should not touch the hot iron, but he did and burned his finger. He doesn't touch the iron anymore, but he had to find out for himself, like I did." He paused. "It's not the way to go," he said.

He seemed absolutely sincere. There seemed no reason to doubt him. Two months later, Wiggins was suspended from the Orioles for having failed a drug test. With this, the commissioner, Peter Ueberroth, suspended Wiggins from baseball "for an indefinite period." Wiggins was then 29 years old and in what should have been his prime as a player. He never returned to the game.

In recent times he had been living on comfortable deferred payments from the Orioles and "dabbling in real estate," said his agent.

What had happened with his battle with drugs? "It's tough," said Attanasio. "You have to remember, 85 percent of all drug users go back to it."

"The lesson in this tragedy," said Jack McKeon, "has to be, you gotta say no to drugs. Drugs'll kill ya. It's just so sad. Wiggy was a nice kid, and he could really create excitement."

STRAWBERRY ATTEMPTS TO DO IT OVER AGAIN

July 14, 1995

COLUMBUS, OHIO — Under the provisions of house, or, rather, hotel arrest, Darryl Strawberry, the newest Columbus Clipper, who arrived Wednesday from the Class A Tampa Yankees, must adhere to a strict routine, mandated by the federal court and administered with the cooperation of another prodigious entity, George M. Steinbrenner. One of the few things Strawberry is allowed by law to do outside of his hotel room is swing at a baseball.

And last night he got his first chance since his modified incarceration to do so on the Triple A level, batting third as the designated hitter for the Clippers against Pawtucket at Cooper Stadium and lining a single to center off a former Mets teammate, Wally Whitehurst, in his first at-bat. By game's end, a 9–3 Clippers victory, Strawberry had added a prodigious three-run homer off the right-field scoreboard against Mike Harley while going 2-for-4 amid a smattering of boos transformed into cheers.

"I finally feel free," Strawberry had said in a personal interview before the game. He did? "I just feel I can be me now, and not try to be someone other people wanted me to be," he said, stuffing a chaw of tobacco in his cheek in the Clippers' small clubhouse. "I don't feel the most important thing is to be a baseball star. The most important thing is for me to be a human being."

He remembered when he first came up to the Mets, in 1983, a 21-year-old expectant superstar. "I wish I could go back and start all over again," he said.

He said he related to something Mickey Mantle said in his news conference Tuesday. "I wasted a lot of my talent, too," said Strawberry, who is expected to spend a week here before the Yankees promote him to the Bronx. "But I've been given another chance to make up for a lot. I'm going to do everything I can to take advantage of it."

He said he understood that there was more to life than baseball, that he had found religion again—he is a reborn, reborn Christian—and that he was playing and living not for earthly pleasures but so that "I might find a place in heaven in Eternal Life."

It was recalled that he had said virtually the same thing a few years ago, after he had come out of drug rehabilitation for the first time. What was different now? "I went back into the world then," he said. "I won't now." He smiled, and his eyes bore a beatific look similar to the one they did then.

And while he says he was a victim of the spotlight, of troubles at home as a boy in Los Angeles, of lack of guidance, he understands, "I'm still responsible for myself."

On the hotel floor where Strawberry has a room, a security guard is stationed all night. Arthur Richman, a Yankee vice president, has a room across the hall, just as he had in Tampa, Florida, when Strawberry was first signed by Steinbrenner three weeks ago, a curious and frequently attacked undertaking. After all, Strawberry was under a 60-day suspension from baseball because of a third violation of his drug program and had played only parts of the last two seasons, being released by the Dodgers and then by the Giants.

Strawberry was also suffering another inconvenience—house arrest—since he was convicted earlier this year of income-tax evasion.

Dick Williams, a Yankee scout and Strawberry's personal batting coach, has a room next door. A probation officer calls Strawberry's room every night after a game. The ballplayer is not allowed meals anywhere but at the ballpark and in his hotel room: the hotel coffee shop and restaurant are off limits.

Strawberry is administered a urine test for drugs almost every day in his hotel room. The hotel operator has a list of about 10 names, people who are allowed to get through to Strawberry. Any other caller must leave a message. A private van picks up Strawberry and his Yankee entourage from the hotel and takes them to the park and brings them back.

In his room, he reads the Bible (as he does in the clubhouse) and talks to his wife, back home in Palm Springs, California. He is allowed to go to Alcoholics Anonymous meetings, and must do community service—he recently visited children at a Shriners Hospital in Tampa and dispensed balls, bats, hats, and good will.

Beyond that, Strawberry offered this advice to the Mets' latest star-hopeful, the 22-year-old pitcher Jason Isringhausen, who arrived yesterday at Shea Stadium: "Be patient: Don't get too excited by being successful; stay away from the wrong crowd—you can tell they're wrong when they do things that aren't normal; and live life on its own terms—don't force things."

This is sound advice for anyone, baseball player or civilian. Without question, however, the person most in need of following such good sense is a good-looking left-handed batter named Darryl Strawberry.

THIS BERNIE IS NOT SOME BANJO HITTER

November 12, 1996

THE TALL, SCHOLARLY LOOKING young man with wire-rim glasses and goatee—but with an obvious bundle of muscle under his blue sweater—strummed a few chords on his electric guitar. He waited on stage at the Bottom Line club in Greenwich Village yesterday afternoon to rehearse with the singer Pete Droge, whom he was to accompany that night on such songs as "Brakeman" and "The House of the Rising Sun."

The tall, scholarly young man admitted to a nervousness for this, his live musical debut—nervousness that, he said, he never quite felt when he was ripping American League pitchers for 29 home runs and 102 runs batted in and a .305 batting average during the 1996 season, and then causing opposing hurlers even more misery as he banged out clutch hits in a pivotal role in the Yankees' climb to a World Series championship.

"Tonight," said Bernie Williams, who would be center stage at the Bottom Line instead of his customary center field in Yankee Stadium, "I know I'll have a lot of butterflies when I come out. I've never done this before, playing before, what? Five hundred people?"

Playing the guitar, that is. But he has gone to bat in crucial situations for the Yankees, and with 60,000 fans screaming. Is that different?

"Very," Williams said. "There's 60,000 people, but you don't see them. You hear them. There's too many to see. And I've batted in public thousands of times. I've only really performed in public just once before, and that was recently on the Conan O'Brien television show, and it was pretty informal stuff."

One similarity between hitting and playing guitar is there must be a combination of aggressiveness and gentleness, Williams said. "It's like you wouldn't approach Roger Clemens and Charlie Hough in the same way," he went on. "Clemens throws heat, so you must try to attack it. Hough throws that fluttery knuckleball, so you have to be much more patient."

Before signing a contract for $16,000 with the Yankees in 1985, Williams, who would study at the University of Puerto Rico, where he held a 3.8 grade-point average as a premed major, had a deep interest in classical guitar. He wasn't sure in which direction he wanted to go. Williams had begun playing the guitar at the same age he began playing baseball, at eight years old, and he developed his guitar skills well enough to attend the Music High School in San Juan.

In years to come, though, he would envy some of his classmates as they continued on around the world playing jazz, blues, and classical music in concert halls. Williams had a problem, however; he was talented in several fields, including the ability to crush a baseball as well as catch one with speed and grace, which he has been doing in Yankee pinstripes for the past five years.

When Williams came onstage, he slowly began to rock with the blaring, amplified group on stage, and by the time he had finished his numbers, he had worked up a sweat. The crowd cheered and even chanted, "Let's go, Yankees!"

"I definitely need a lot of work," Williams said later. But Droge's assessment was this: "He smoked."

"One comparison between playing baseball and playing the guitar," Williams had said, "is the work ethic. To be good, you have to be disciplined in both. In baseball, you practice and practice to get a quality at-bat, hitting the ball level and getting good wood on it. But in baseball, you get more than one chance to hit in a game. The difference in performing in music is that all your mistakes have to be made in practice. You only get one shot when you're on stage."

His baseball came to such a point last month that after he won Game 1 of the postseason series against the Orioles with a leadoff, eleventh-inning home run, and created similar havoc in other games, he was approached by Joe DiMaggio under the stands. "Good to meet you," the legendary Yankee said to him. "You're having a great year. Keep it up."

"I couldn't believe it," Williams recalled. "I talked to Joe DiMaggio. And he actually talked to me!"

But that thrill—and the loud pleasure he experienced last night—were topped by the parade for the Yankees after the Series triumph, a blizzard of affection in which cheering, confetti-flinging fans were wall-to-wall for blocks.

"I've never seen anything like that in my life," Williams said. "Counting the movies, man."

BABE RUTH AND JOHN DILLINGER

October 15, 1973

HE HAD THE MAKINGS of a coach's dream. He was strong and fast and dexterous and certainly quick-witted. If you look at some of the old pictures of him, pictures that show both his profile and his face front, you see he was a clean-cut-looking chap. He had neatly trimmed sideburns, was clean shaven, and he wouldn't be an embarrassment on a road trip because he would wear tie and suit.

A rare photo of him on the Martinsville, Indiana, town team, in the spring of 1924, shows that he also looked spiffy in a pinstriped baseball uniform; his peaked cap had a jaunty cock to it, revealing a youthful zeal, a kind of run-through-the-wall-for-you quality that coaches usually like.

"He was a good all-around ballplayer. He was a good batter, good fielder, and fast—he could steal anything," recalled his brother-in-law, Emmett Hancock.

He was 5′7¼″, weighed a lithe 150 pounds, and a biographer believes that he may have been fascinated by the careers of both Ty Cobb and Babe Ruth.

Cobb, whom he may have identified with more closely than Ruth because of the resemblance in physical build, was a daring competitor, in a rough-and-ready era.

Possibly, though, he also identified with Ruth, for both had some troubles with the law. Both were sent to reformatories. Ruth was even termed "incorrigible," but of course we know he was not.

The fellow we are talking about now began to distinguish himself on the reformatory baseball team, as a second baseman. Strangely, Ruth did the same at St. Mary's and was finally allowed to pursue a professional baseball career.

The governor of Indiana, then a man named Harry Leslie, had seen our fellow play ball in the reformatory's yard and remarked, "That kid ought to be playing major league baseball."

He overheard the comment and used it to get himself transferred to another prison, in Michigan City. Supposedly, it was because that prison had a better ballclub.

However, he was more concerned with being among men he could better learn his trade from, such as Three-Fingered Jack Hamilton (no relation to Mordecai "Three Finger" Brown of the Chicago Cubs). He was transferred to Michigan City but he never again played baseball.

The only reason for comparing a Ruth, say, with our fellow, is to observe the quirky working of Fate, and how careers may run parallel for a while and then dramatically diverge.

Our fellow did not become, as the governor of Indiana had thought possible, a big-league baseball player.

He did, though, achieve national celebrity. In fact, in 1933 a poll in an Indianapolis high school determined that more students knew who he was than knew who Franklin Delano Roosevelt was.

He did use his athletic skills in his business, however. He ran fast. He was daring. He was strong. He was clever. And some were so in awe of his leaping abilities (perhaps perfected in practicing the double play) that he was called by some "the Vaulter" (which was also a pun). And he did leap and scale barriers five to 12 feet high.

Funny, too, his first partner in his business was a man who had been a local umpire, but he was not a player, and this helped make him a rather bitter fellow. He had webbed fingers, and he felt he had been handed a raw deal. A major motion picture based on our fellow's life is now in the nation's theaters. And there have been several biographies of his exploits. All this despite his rather foreshortened career. He was in the headlines for a total of only 15 months. His career was short but meteoric, like Pistol Pete Reiser's.

On July 22, 1934, at the young age of 32, our fellow, bankrobber John Dillinger, was gunned down by FBI men in Chicago.

Ironically, Babe Ruth also retired the next season.

• • •

(The writer wishes to acknowledge the cooperation of Joseph Pinkston, coauthor of *Dillinger: A Short and Violent Life*, published by McGraw-Hill, and Jay Robert Nash, author of *Bloodletters and Badmen*, published by M. Evans, for much of the above information.)

ONE FOR ELI YALE

November 23, 1985

FOR THE 102ND ANNUAL Harvard-Yale game at the Yale Bowl in New Haven this afternoon, the weatherman said there was a chance of rain, but not necessarily a torrent. It seems unlikely that it would be anything like the 1932 Harvard-Yale game, which was played in one of the worst rainstorms in New Haven history. It rained so hard for so long that even Babe Ruth left the game early.

The *New York Times* of November 20, 1932, reported the details of the game, a 19-0 victory for Yale, highlighted by Walter Levering's touchdown runs of 45 and 55 yards. Following the account of the game, there appeared a small item, which read: "Babe Ruth sat in the downpour with Mrs. Ruth until even his massive physique could not stand it any longer. He left in the fourth quarter totally unnoticed. He was just another bedraggled figure heading for the exits."

Someone who will never forget that game and keeps that clipping among his Yale memorabilia is Milton White, professor emeritus of English at Miami University in Oxford, Ohio. He was a 17-year-old freshman at Yale in 1932.

He remembers the days leading up to the big game, and the excitement. "I wasn't a great sports fan, but, after all, this was the Harvard-Yale game, and there would only be two that I could go to as an undergraduate," he said. "I didn't think I could attend the two at Harvard. I mean, it was the Depression, and I was very poor—destitute, I guess you'd say—and my father, who was a merchant-tailor in Springfield, Massachusetts, had saved hard to send me to Yale. I thought I'd never be able to afford to go to Boston for the game."

Freshman White was supposed to have a date for the game. A girl he knew in Springfield was going to come down for it, and earlier in the week he had arranged with a woman who worked in a local florist to buy a white chrysanthemum for 35¢. "But my date conked out at the last minute," said White. He had also planned a double-date at the game with his roommate and his date, but they decided to stay indoors because of the rain. He gave the chrysanthemum to his roommate for his girl, and young White went off to the game alone. He had never known it to rain so hard. Wearing a yellow slicker and a yellow rain hat to match, he waited in the rain for a trolley, and dodged the spray of taxicabs. Finally, the trolley clanged into view, and he boarded it to the Yale Bowl.

On the way, he saw parties going on in the warmth of rooms in dormitories and apartments. Those people were simply not going out in this rain. But Milton White was determined to attend the game.

When he arrived at the Yale Bowl, he trudged through puddles and sloshed down the aisle to a seat near the 30-yard line.

"I remember that the stadium looked pretty empty," he said.

He sat down on the soaking bench. The rain had dripped from the collar of his slicker down the wool jacket he wore underneath and made him uncomfortable.

"I've always hated the smell of wet wool," he said.

Most of the people at the game were huddled around the 50-yard line. "I was too shy to go there at first, but after a while I said, 'Oh, why not?'"

So he moved down and took a seat closer to the 50-yard-line, a solitary figure in the pouring rain. He had been sitting there only a moment or so when he felt someone tapping him on the shoulder.

"You don't want to sit alone," the man behind him said. "Come sit with us."

The man was with a woman, and they were sitting "sort of off to the side," recalled White. The couple held a large strip of linoleum to protect them from the rain. White, even through rain-streaked glasses, recognized him immediately. "I know you, you're Babe Ruth!" he said.

"He had a wonderful smile," White recalled, "and he introduced me to his wife. I was aghast. She said, 'Come on under, you don't want to get wet.'" The couple shifted the linoleum in order to extend a piece of it for White. At about this time, the Yale and the Harvard teams came sloshing onto the field, and the small crowd cheered. The Yale Band struck up "Boola Boola."

"The game was just about to begin, and Babe Ruth lifted a gallon jug from under the bench," said White. "He poured something into a paper cup for himself and he poured one for me. They looked like whisky sours. He handed me a cup. 'To Eli Yale,' he said. My hand was shaking. 'Eli Yale,' I said. Babe Ruth grinned at me. We raised our cups and drank.

"I remember that he seemed somehow to understand my loneliness, and I wondered if he was lonely, too, even being so famous. But I never dared asked him anything like that. In fact, I don't really remember anything else about the game, except that Yale won."

He said he didn't even recall when he left, but it was probably when his companions departed in the fourth quarter with their strip of linoleum that had protected the three of them against the rain.

YOGI: BASEBALL'S ODDEST MARVEL

October 12, 1973

ANYONE AWARE of Yogi Berra's history will not be stunned that he has come out of the National League pennant race smelling like a phoenix.

Berra, too, is a mythological bird who seems to immolate himself, and then emerge reborn, bigger and better and luckier than ever.

As manager of the New York Mets, he was on the brink of occupational disaster. His team this season was in last place in the East Division as late as July 8, and 12 games behind the leaders. Incredibly, the Mets went on to win the pennant.

Return with us now, to those thrilling days of yesteryear, when Berra began his daring, death-defying feats of flying past one great opportunity only to land smack in the pot of gold at the end of the rainbow.

The St. Louis Cardinals wanted to sign two local standouts, Joe Garagiola and Lawrence Peter Berra (even then known as "Yogi"—meaning, in his neighborhood, an odd fellow). Garagiola received a $500 bonus; Berra wanted same. St. Louis offered $300. Berra said no. The Cards forgot about him. Enter the Yankees, who signed him.

During Yogi's 17 full seasons as a major leaguer, Berra virtually got rich on the Yankees' 14 World Series checks alone. The Cardinals, in that time, won no pennants.

In Berra's rookie year, he was behind the plate in the 1947 World Series. But the Dodgers, with Jackie Robinson, created such base-running havoc for him that he was relegated to right field. Yet in later years he became a Hall of Fame catcher.

One of the most memorable moments of luck and pluck in an athlete's life came for Berra in the shadowy late afternoon of September 28, 1951. He was catching what was most certainly going to be Allie Reynolds' second shutout of the season.

With two out in the ninth inning, Boston slugger Ted Williams popped up. Berra tossed off his mask, nestled under the ball. And dropped it. Almost diabolically, Williams popped up behind home plate again! Berra, in his comical, knock-kneed, dumpy manner, dizzily circled under the ball. But now made proper use of his angelic second chance. No-hitter.

He was named manager of the Yankees in 1964, and the story of how he won a pennant but lost the World Series and, therefore, his job, is an oft-told folk tale.

Few wondered then what might become of the seemingly sad little figure named Yogi, since in his ungrammatical, stumbling way he had amassed much money from shrewd investments.

But he did arise as coach of the New York Mets. His baseball acumen was hardly the sole reason for his hiring. It was thought by the Mets that dear, legendary Yogi would draw fans, even as a first-base coach. Besides, nice things often unwittingly happened to Yogi. For example, when a pedagogical and too logical manager tried to "correct" Yogi's habit of swinging at bad balls, Berra responded, "I can't hit and think at the same time."

And nice things soon did happen to the Mets, whether it was totally Yogi's talisman that did it is a moot point. The once-absurd Mets miraculously (do you know a better word?) won the World Series in 1969.

Last spring, Gil Hodges suddenly died. The Mets needed a manager quick. Berra was chosen, amid moans of many who still considered Berra a fortuitous buffoon, at best.

This season, the Mets were thought to have pennant possibilities. But a series of injuries to key players such as Cleon Jones, Bud Harrelson, Rusty Staub, John Milner, Jerry Grote, and Jon Matlack hurt immeasurably. Berra's critics grew louder. Berra maintained his funny-faced aplomb. "I'm doin' the best wit' what I got," he continued to say.

There was no word of encouragement from the front office. In fact, Willie Mays, the darling of the owners, came and went as he pleased, thus kicking harder the underpinnings of Berra's authority. The manager withstood.

His wounded players returned to full flower. The Mets made a run for the division title. Hits weirdly began to fall in; a Mets' misjudged fly ball mysteriously was blown back toward him, and he caught it; the other team puzzlingly ran into each other in the field. Berra's magic was again on the beam.

All along, he pretended no sagacity. "The game is 50-50," says Berra. "I remember near the end of the season I replaced Jerry Koosman with Tug McGraw. I come back to the dugout, and a fan says, 'Yogi, did you do right?' I says back, 'Dunno, we'll see in a minute.'"

There is no better example of Berra's uncanny ability to survive than when he was the Met first-base coach. He thought he could do greater service for runners if he watched the bag and not the hitter. So Berra stood astraddle on the coach's line, back to batter. Hodges pleaded: either watch the batter or at least wear a protective cap liner.

"I never felt any danger," recalls Berra, "so I stayed doin' it my way. Oh, a couple times line drives whistled through my legs, but dat was all."

MCDOUGALD, ONCE A QUIET YANKEE, NOW LIVES IN QUIET WORLD

July 10, 1994

IT IS A SILENT SUMMER for Gil McDougald; they are all silent summers.

Once, summertime for Gil McDougald, a standout Yankee infielder in the 1950s, was full of the sweet sounds of baseball—balls being struck, the chatter and laughter of teammates, the roar of the crowd. He can no longer hear those sounds, although his wife, Lucille, says, "He can hear them internally."

Gil McDougald is deaf. He gradually lost his hearing during his playing days, after a freak accident in batting practice in which he was struck by a batted ball. Ironically, this occurred just two years before the famous incident in which he cracked a line drive off the right eye of Herb Score, a Cleveland Indians pitcher.

Until that moment against Cleveland, in the first inning of a game in Municipal Stadium on the night of May 7, 1957, Score appeared on the way to becoming one of baseball's best pitchers ever, and McDougald seemed to have a long career ahead of him.

"I heard the thud of the ball hitting his head and then saw him drop and lie there, bleeding, and I froze," McDougald recalled. "Someone hollered for me to run to first. When Score was taken off the field on a stretcher, I was sick to my stomach. I didn't want to play anymore."

But Casey Stengel, his manager, insisted he continue. "He said, 'You're getting paid to play.' And while that seems harsh, it was right. It's like getting right back on a horse after you've been thrown.

"But I said that if Herb loses his eye, I'm quitting baseball."

McDougald remembers that Score's mother called and told him it wasn't his fault, that it was just an accident. He called Score in the hospital, to apologize, to offer his heartfelt best wishes, and kept in regular touch with him.

Score returned to action the next season, his eye healed. But in many ways, neither McDougald nor Score was ever the same again.

After the Score incident, fans in cities that the Yankees visited began to boo McDougald. "Some people would holler, 'Killer,'" he said. "Funny thing is, as bad as I felt, I went on a hitting spree. I can't explain it."

Yesterday, Old-Timers' Day at Yankee Stadium, McDougald, now 66 years old, chose not to attend, even though the theme involved his years as a Yankee. It was the 45th anniversary of the beginning in 1949 of the Casey Stengel era, and the first of Stengel's record five straight World Series championship teams, three of which McDougald was a member.

McDougald played superbly in those garlanded baseball days as a feared clutch hitter and a regular second baseman, third baseman, and shortstop, wherever Stengel felt he needed him on a particular day. In McDougald's 53 games in eight World Series over his 10-year career, he started every game at one of those three positions.

"It is too frustrating and too exhausting for Gil to be around the other players and trying to understand all the banter and the reminiscences," said Lucille McDougald. "He was content to watch it on television at home."

It was during batting practice one afternoon that McDougald himself had been struck by a batted ball. He was standing behind a screen at second base talking with the Yankee coach, Frank Crosetti.

"I saw a ball lying on the ground nearby and reached to pick it up, my head going just beyond the screen," he said. "Just then Bob

Cerv hit a ball that hit me in the ear. I collapsed and everyone came running over. They carried me off the field, and I was out of action for a few games.

"The doctors told me I'd be all right. Well, I wasn't. The blow had broken a hearing tube. At first it just affected one ear, my left. One time I'm getting needled by some fan at third base, and I turned to Rizzuto at short and said, 'Too bad I didn't get hit in the right ear, then I wouldn't have to hear this guy.'"

But the hearing got progressively worse, although it had nothing to do with his leaving baseball after the 1960 season, at age 32.

"I just got tired of the travel, and the attitude of the baseball people," he said. "I started at $5,500 a year with the Yankees, and then was making $37,500 at the end. But they acted like they owned you and that they were giving you the moon and stars."

He had a family with four children at the time, and felt he needed more money to support it and saw a way to do it through a business of his own. He had already begun a dry cleaning business, and it was doing nicely.

"Some of my teammates, and others asked, 'How can you quit baseball?' No one thought I'd follow through. But I found it was easy."

Because of his loss of hearing, McDougald says he hasn't answered a telephone in 10 years. Because of the handicap, he sold his share in the building maintenance company he owned, which employed 2,200 people on the East Coast, and he was forced into early retirement.

"When I couldn't use the phone, it became a real pain in the neck," he said. He keeps an interest in baseball, however, and while he watches some of it on television, he says he doesn't miss the voices of the announcers—except for his old teammates, Phil Rizzuto and Tony Kubek.

"The others just talk so much that it wears you out," said McDougald. "I'd just as soon watch the action and draw my own conclusions."

And what does he see? "I see a lot of guys making a million dollars," he said, and laughed. "There are some very good ballplayers, but some of the things they do are pretty funny. Like if a pitcher throws close to a batter, he faints. When he wakes up, he charges the mound."

McDougald sat at the kitchen table in his sprawling, 22-room Spanish colonial house where he lives with his wife and, depending on who happens to be staying or visiting, some or all of his seven children, seven grandchildren, and one great-grandchild. He and Lucille adopted three of their children, of mixed races, later in life through Catholic Charities.

"We had four children to begin with, and then when they all grew up and left the house, Lucille and I started getting lonely," he said, "so when we were about 40 years old, we set about to adopt the other kids."

In a white short-sleeve pullover and blue jeans and white sneakers, he appears as trim as in his playing days. Indeed, at 180 pounds, the 6′ McDougald weighs about the same as when he was playing third base, shortstop, and second base for the Yankees, from 1951, when he came up to the majors with Mickey Mantle, through 1960. He hit over .300 twice, and played an important role in the eight World Series the Yankees played in over his 10 years with them.

"He was a money player," said Saul Rogovin, who pitched for the White Sox in that era. "He would hurt you in the late innings."

Through the window behind McDougald is another large, white, columned house like his and, just beyond that, the ocean, sparkling in the morning sunlight, the waves hitting the beach with a sound of which McDougald is now unaware.

There remains an angularity to his ruddy face and body, and one is reminded of that odd, open, wide stance of his at the plate, head cocked to one side, like, well, like he was listening to a faraway sound.

"An awkward man, a wonderful man," Stengel said about him.

McDougald laughed now, recalling a move that Stengel used to make: "Casey always knew when a man was ready to pinch-hit or not. And I could read him like a book. He'd come by on the bench and stand and look you right in the eye. Like he'd stop in front of Bobby Brown, and he'd say something like, 'Bauer,' or 'Woodling, grab a bat.' Still looking at Brown. Casey was a hunch manager. No statistics for him. He'd look at a guy and get the feeling. It was funny."

There is no problem, to be sure, with McDougald's speech, and he responds when questions are written out for him, or, on occasion, when he reads lips, which is laborious for him: "You have to concentrate so hard that it begins to give you a headache," he said.

Sitting with Lucille at the kitchen table, McDougald recently tried to field a visitor's question. He knit his brow, trying to read the lips. "What did you say?" he said.

Lucille said, slowly, "He said, 'Did Stengel ever give you advice about hitting?'"

He recalled a moment in the fifth game in his first World Series, against the New York Giants in 1951. The bases were loaded, and he was about to bat. Stengel called him back to the dugout.

"Casey said, 'Hit one out.'" McDougald said with a laugh. "And wouldn't you know, I went up to the plate and did. It was in the Polo Grounds, I hit a fly ball that carried about 260 feet down that short left-field line, just one of those Chinese homers, but it cleared the fence."

At the time, it was only the third bases-loaded home run in World Series history.

McDougald batted .306 during that regular season of 1951, the only Yankee batter to hit .300 or better, and was named the American League's Rookie of the Year, playing second base and third, ahead of either Jerry Coleman or Bobby Brown. He also hit 14 homers, one more than another rookie on the team, Mickey Mantle.

"I remember our first spring training together, and you couldn't believe the publicity for Mickey," he said. "He was in the newspapers and magazines more than the president. From that point forward, his life was never his own. That's what stardom does. It was like what I saw with Joe DiMaggio. Nineteen fifty-one was his last season as a ballplayer, and I don't think I saw him come down to eat in the hotel one time. He stayed in his room because he'd be so bothered by people.

"Mickey was a 19-year-old kid from Oklahoma. New York seemed like a huge place to him. I was different. I was from San Francisco, 22 years old, and had a year of college. He began hanging out with Billy Martin, and every night was a party. I roomed with Hank Bauer, and it wasn't the same for us.

"But Mickey had different pressures than me, being the star he was. I saw him on television recently, and he talked about the drinking helping to relieve the pressure. It was very sad for me, knowing Mickey as I do, liking him, seeing what's happened."

He remembers the wild things some of his teammates did, including Ryne Duren, the pitcher. "Once I saw him drink two bottles of vodka out of both sides of his mouth," said McDougald. "I thought, *He's crazy.*"

Duren is an alcoholic, who later rehabilitated, and now counsels others about their drinking problems. "I saw Ryne at a golf tournament a few years back," said McDougald, "and he looked beautiful."

McDougald shied away from other activities, such as dinners and banquets, because he found them frustrating, and somewhat embarrassing, because he was unable to hear. "I'd just sit there like a dummy," he said.

Over the years, he had grown more disturbed as the hearing began to wane. And when his family gets together, he still grows impatient with not being able to share in the conversations—"especially the jokes," he said—and so may retire upstairs where he can work on business interests he retains, or check the stock market, in which he remains active, or view television or read a book or magazine or newspaper, seeking to "keep up with the world." Or he may practice his putting on the small artificial green in his den.

McDougald still regularly plays tennis and golf. In a recent, genial dialogue with Ottilie Lucas, the blind wife of his nephew, they debated handicaps. She said she'd rather be blind than deaf because with loss of eyesight she is more sensitive to the world around her and so appreciates it more.

McDougald argued that he'd rather be deaf than blind. "If I was blind," he said, "I couldn't play golf."

At one point, McDougald considered getting a hearing implant but it wouldn't do much good, he was told, since he can occasionally hear sounds but the sounds are fragmented and he can make no sense out of them.

He remains in touch with some of his old teammates, like Rizzuto and Yogi Berra, and remembers his biggest thrill being his first game in Yankee Stadium.

"The ballpark seemed so big to me," he said, "and the roar of the crowd was overwhelming."

He even occasionally gets a note from Herb Score. "He pitched again after I hit him, but he was never the same again," said McDougald. "I could see him recoiling after he threw, rather than following through as he had before. But he's done very well, as an announcer for the Indians, and I'm glad to see it."

McDougald had done well, too, succeeding in business and then, for seven years, coaching the Fordham University baseball team while still active in his business. He quit coaching baseball when he could no longer hear the crack of the bat.

"You know, there used to be a sportswriter for the *New York Times* named John Drebinger, who covered the Yankees," said McDougald. "He wore a hearing aid. We'd mock him all the time, and play tricks on him. He'd come over in the clubhouse, and we'd be moving our lips, as if we were talking. He'd beat that squawk box in his ear, then he'd turn it up. And then we'd all start laughing. He'd say, 'Why you dirty so-and-sos.'" And McDougald laughed.

"And now it's happened to me," he said. "But you go on, you learn to live with it. You make your adjustments. There's still a lot to live for, and love."

Gil McDougald turned and looked out of the window, his face to the rays of sun that streamed in, silent and welcome, like the summertime.

FOR MCDOUGALD,
THE MIRACLE OF SOUND

January 4, 1995

THERE WAS A TENSION at breakfast that Gil McDougald, the standout infielder on the great Yankee teams of the 1950s, tried not to acknowledge, a tension that had been building since November. That was when he had undergone the operation to insert a cochlear implant behind his right ear with the hope of being able to hear again.

McDougald, silver-haired at age 66, but still looking trim in his tan turtleneck, sat in a booth yesterday in the East Bay Restaurant on First Avenue with his wife, Lucille, and one of their daughters, Denise Costigan, one of their seven grown children, in fact.

The McDougalds had taken the nearly two-hour train ride from their home in Spring Lake, New Jersey, and would be going across the street to Bellevue Hospital. There, McDougald would be programmed for a hearing apparatus, and would learn if this operation, a relatively recent and delicate procedure, was a success or not.

McDougald had gradually gone deaf in both ears after a freak-ish accident in which he was hit above the right ear by a line drive during batting practice in 1955. For the last 20 years and more, he has been nearly stone deaf, able to make out some sounds, but no intelligible words, though he could lip read to a limited extent.

"When I sent out my Christmas cards, I wrote that it would be wonderful if the procedure was a success and Gil could hear again," Lucille McDougald was saying. "I showed him the card before I sent it out. He said, 'You can't say that. You have to accept the fact that there are no guarantees with this operation. It's like baseball. You can't get too excited, otherwise you'll blow the whole thing.'

"I said, 'I'm the author of this card, and I'll say what I want.'"

McDougald laughed. "So many people have called and written that they are praying for me that I'm concerned," he said. "I mean, if the procedure doesn't work, they'll blame me for their loss of faith."

McDougald had come to this point after an article last summer had described his silent life, in which, as Lucille described it, he heard the roar of the crowd "only internally."

The article described how McDougald, unable to talk on the telephone anymore, had to sell his share in the building maintenance business he owned; how he stopped attending functions with old friends and old ballplayers—some, like Yogi Berra and Phil Rizzuto and Mickey Mantle, were teammates in all or most of the eight World Series he played in over his 10-year career—because he was unable to participate in the jokes and give-and-take; and how, at family functions, McDougald would leave the table in frustration at being unable to hear the conversation.

Several doctors contacted him and told him about the implant surgery and about Dr. Noel Cohen, head of otolaryngology at New York University Medical Center. Reluctant at first to subject himself to further disappointment, McDougald finally called Dr. Cohen.

Cohen determined that McDougald was a good candidate for the operation because he retained a tiny bit of residual hearing of tones. But McDougald postponed the operation until the winter. "I didn't want to give up my summer of golf," he said. "I had waited this long, I could wait a little longer."

"Everyone," said Cohen, with a smile, "has his priorities."

The implant is a receiver that is wired to an electrode, which stimulates the cochlea, an organ in the inner ear. The implant cannot restore normal hearing because it does not amplify sound, instead converting sound into electronic signals. Its effectiveness varies from patient to patient.

After the operation, Cohen pronounced the implant a success. But it would take about six weeks for McDougald to heal, and then he had to visit an audiologist, Betsy Bromberg, at neighboring Bellevue, for an evaluation of his hearing and to have the apparatus programmed. How well would this work? Would McDougald be able to hear?

In the office, McDougald sat at a desk with a computer on it. Bromberg sat across from him. His wife and daughter sat within arms' length.

A small microphone was set behind his ear, and a transmitter with a magnet was placed over the site of the implant. A cable was extended from the microphone to a speech processor the size of a hand calculator that can be worn on a belt or placed in a breast pocket.

Then Bromberg began the test that would determine how much McDougald's hearing had improved.

Bromberg covered her mouth with a sheet of paper so he could not lip read.

"Tell me," she said, "what you hear."

She said, "aah." He hesitated. "Aah," he answered. She went, "eeeh." He said, "eeeh."

"Hello," she said. "Hello," he said. "I'm going to count to five," she said. "Do you hear me?"

"Oh, yeah!" he said. "Wow! This is exciting!"

His wife and daughter stared, hardly moving.

Bromberg wrote down four words on a pad of paper, and said them: "football," "sidewalk," "cowboy," and "outside." "Now, Gil," she said, "I'm going to mix up the word order and cover my mouth and you tell me the word I say."

"Cowboy," she said. "Cowboy," he said. "Outside," she said, "Outside," he said. And then he began to flush. Tears welled in his eyes.

"This is the first time in…" Lucille said and then choked up, unable to finish her sentence. "It's unbelievable."

"It's a miracle," said Denise.

Both began crying.

Bromberg said, "It's okay. Everybody cries at times like this." And then mother and daughter embraced. And they hugged Gil. And they hugged Bromberg, and hugged the director of the unit, Susan Waltzman, who had been observing.

"It's great," said McDougald. Then he sat down. "I have a problem," he said. "My voice, gee, it sounds terrible."

"You haven't heard your voice in about 25 years," said Bromberg. "You'll get used to it."

She went through some more adjustments, and then gave McDougald a lesson in how to operate the various components. She told him how he will have some problems, especially in trying to hear a companion on a busy street, or someone at the far end of a noisy dinner table, or someone in another room.

In time, he might also be able to hear on the telephone.

"It's really a surprise," said McDougald. "I mean, I really didn't expect..." He paused, trying to find the words to express his feeling. "They've turned the music on," he said.

Last night, the McDougald household was bursting with children and grandchildren. "Everyone," said Lucille McDougald, "has come to watch grandpa hear."

III.

ATOP THE HILL

THE GOOSE IN HIS OLD NEST

June 4, 1988

WE REMEMBER HIM with the Yankees, for six years from 1978 through 1983, when Goose Gossage was possibly the most fearsome man in baseball.

He was built more like a walrus than a goose, big and beefy, wearing a drooping mustache the ends of which were as long as tusks. His ball cap was pulled down so far on his face that hitters saw only the lower parts of his eyes.

He was 6'4" and 225 pounds, and when he strode in from the bullpen with the game on the line, climbed the mound—"In the crunch, that's when I go crazy," he once said—and unfurled, he released smoke, and somewhere in that smoke, speeding toward the plate, was an aspirin tablet.

At one point when he was still with the Yankees, the Goose, that most menacing creature, was asked: Was there anyone who intimidated him?

"Yes," he said. "Waiters in New York restaurants." Anywhere in particular? "All over."

He recalled this the other night in Shea Stadium, where he was in town with the Chicago Cubbies, with whom the Goose, now in his 17th season in the big leagues and who will be 37 years old next month, still attempts to strike fear in the hearts of batsmen, sometimes with success, and, as on Thursday, sometimes without.

He entered the game in the tenth inning with the Cubs ahead 1–0 and gave up a run on two singles and a stolen base to allow

99

the Mets to tie the game. He left after pitching a scoreless eleventh, but he opened the opportunity for the Mets to win, which they did in the thirteenth, on Howard Johnson's solo home run.

"The game is over," Gossage said afterward. "You go on to the next one."

Despite Thursday night's game, he remains effective, having been credited with six saves this season, tied for fifth in the league. He is striking out an average of one batter per inning, as he has for much of his career, though his fastball isn't the express it once was, and he relies more than ever on his slider.

He had been traded last winter from San Diego to the Cubs, and says he's happy to be in Chicago where baseball tradition is great, the fans are knowledgeable, and pleasingly obnoxious, unlike "laid-back San Diego," but like, he noted, fans in New York. "I don't mind being hooted," he said. "It makes me you feel like it's real baseball."

He says that he'll "always have a soft spot" for New York and that his six years with the Yankees were among "the happiest of my big-league career."

It would seem that absence just might make the heart grow fonder, for he had problems in New York, with Billy Martin, with George Steinbrenner, with the citizenry, but, he says, he lived and learned.

"In New York," he said, "everything is a struggle. You go to a restaurant, it's a fight. You walk down the street, and people bump you. I took my kids to a merry-go-round in a mall in Paramus, New Jersey, and normally people would stand in line, but here they're pushin' and shovin'." What did the Goose do? "I started pushin' and shovin', too. You gotta stand your ground. Then you drive through all that traffic, and by the time you get to the ballpark you're mentally prepared for the battle."

Nor did things get much easier in the ballpark.

"With the Yankees in those days, it was a veteran team, and everybody ragged everybody," he said, smiling. "Nothing was sacred. I mean, if your mother messed up, they'd get on your mother." Not Mother Goose, too? "Yep. That's how they were—

Catfish and Mickey Rivers and Piniella and Nettles and Reggie and Munson.

"When I first got to the Yankees, there was a lot of pressure on me. I took Sparky Lyle's job, and he had won the Cy Young Award the year before. We started the season on the road, and I think I lost three games. So now we come into Yankee Stadium, and I'm called into the game, and Munson walks out to the mound and says, 'Well, how you gonna lose this one?'

"I looked at him. 'Just go back and catch the ball.'

"He said, 'I haven't been catching many lately.'

"Another time I'm getting ready to pitch, and Munson calls time out and comes out and says, 'Check Rivers.' I look around, and Mickey is in a three-point stance, like a track runner, with his butt to me, ready to chase down the ball.

"Then one time I'm called in from the bullpen in center, and I climb in the car, the door opens, and Rivers jumps on the hood and spread-eagles himself. 'Don't let him in the game!' he hollers. 'Don't let him in the game!' I roll down the window, and holler, 'Get off that car or we'll run you over!'

"It was like when you're a kid, and you're having fun. That's the way baseball should be played."

But some of it began to pale for the Goose, and in 1983 he opted for free agency. He had said he no longer desired to play for Steinbrenner, that he was embarrassed when the Yankees' principal owner apologized to Yankee fans about not winning the 1981 World Series and management "started messing with the lineup and messing around every other way, too—all this off-the-game junk, in elevators and that stuff."

But in San Diego, he apparently began to appreciate the Yankees' principal owner. The Goose criticized San Diego management when it banned beer in the clubhouse after games and accused it of wanting "choir boys." He also gave no stars in his review of the hamburgers sold by Joan Kroc, owner of the Padres and the McDonald's fast-food chain.

"George," says Gossage, "wanted to win. I couldn't say that about Joan Kroc."

So New York now is a fond memory for Goose Gossage.

Even, he was asked, Steinbrenner's remark in 1982 that the Goose should do more pitching and less quacking?

He laughed and tugged at his baseball cap.

"Even that," he said.

ERA ENDS: GATOR SAYS "SO LONG"

July 13, 1989

RON GUIDRY, the suddenly former Yankee pitcher, had a smile on his lean face, though, at times, in the glare of the lights of the television cameras at the news conference, one could see a little moistness rimming his eyes, and perhaps belying some of his words.

He was saying good-bye to all those memorable yesterdays and would begin greeting all those uncertain tomorrows.

He recalled when he was a rookie in 1976 and thought he had made the club, only to be told that he was going to be sent back down to the minor leagues. He didn't understand how some of the veterans wanted so much to hang on. "Now I know how hard it is to let go," he said, "but I understand that you can't stand in the way of the young guys."

Gator, or Louisiana Lightnin', as he has been called, stood yesterday afternoon in the front of a room at Yankee Stadium and announced his retirement from baseball, one month short of his 39th birthday. He was situated between his wife, Bonnie, and three children, Jamie (12), Brandon (nine), and Danielle (four), on one side, and Bob Quinn and Syd Thrift, Yankee executives, on the other.

In Yankee history, in terms of victories for a pitcher, he was also situated just below Ford, Ruffing, and Gomez, and, with 170 victories, ahead of Shawkey and Stottlemyre and Pennock and Hoyt and Reynolds and Chesbro and Raschi and Lopat. This was, after

13 seasons in the big leagues, some company that he'll be keeping for all time.

This spring, Guidry looked good, firing 90 mph fastballs and biting sliders, which recalled such times as the 1978 season, when he was the pitcher of the year with a 25–3 record on a world championship team, the club's last.

But this spring he began suffering elbow problems, underwent surgery, and then was sent to the Columbus farm club to try to work his way back into the Yankee starting rotation. And minor league batters knocked him about.

So on this day, the last day of all his Yankee yesterdays, he wore a light-blue sport jacket and a white shirt open at the collar and a gold medal with *NY* encircled on it. With neat black mustache, he looked as he always has, thin as a pencil, and one could see him again raring back in that familiar fashion and hurling a pitch an arsonist would be proud of.

He recalled the day in '78 when he struck out 18 against the Angels, and had "nothing" in the bullpen. After the first inning, in which a line drive "nearly killed me," he asked his catcher, Thurman Munson, "Whattya think?" Munson said, "I think you oughta say a prayer." Guidry didn't do much better in the second inning. But then, Guidry recalled, he began to get the ball past the hitters, and, after the third inning, he said, "I got my first indication that this was goin' to be somethin' special when I overheard Thurman say to our trainer, Gene Monahan, 'I need another pad.'"

This drew laughs from the gathered reporters, and from his family. Guidry got more laughs when he talked about being with the Yankees in all the days of turmoil, when it seemed management was always fighting with the players—there were Piniella and Hunter and Jackson and Lyle and Nettles and Gossage—and the players were always fighting with management, and among themselves.

Here was Guidry, this gentleman, this crowd favorite, this quiet professional, who did nothing in his 13 years but distinguish himself, smiling, recalling, saying he was going to go back to his home in Louisiana and build a barn and sit on a tractor and, maybe, oh, become a hunting guide, "because it's only baseball and hunting that I know anything about."

It was going to be fine, though he would miss New York, miss the game, miss "the guys," his teammates.

He said he felt deeply but doesn't often show emotion, his wife sometimes calling him "a walking zombie."

Then someone asked Bonnie Guidry how she felt, and she said "a little happy, a little sad—mostly sad." And she began to sob. "But I still think Ron can pitch," she said. "And this will be the Yankees' loss."

Listening, Guidry did not raise his head. He seemed to be thinking, yes, I can still win in the big leagues.

A teammate, Dave Righetti, stood watching in a corner, respectfully, finger to his cheek. Later he'd say Guidry was his role model, and one day this will happen to him, but he'd rather not think about it.

He said this was definitely the end of an era. "But maybe with Donnie and Pags and guys like that we'll start a new era," Righetti said.

As Righetti spoke, Guidry and his family were stepping into an elevator, and leaving Yankee Stadium, and leaving all those echoes of all those cheers.

FORTY YEARS LATER, LARSEN STILL DELIGHTS IN HIS PERFECTION AND HIS LUCK

July 28, 1996

IT WAS A PLEASANT fall day nearly 40 years ago. Nothing, it seemed, out of the ordinary. A weekday afternoon, October 8, with leaves turning on the Chicago streets. My father had picked me up from high school, and we were headed to a factory outlet in regard to some business. As I got into the car, he had the radio on. It was the fifth game of the World Series between the Yankees and Dodgers at Yankee Stadium.

"The Yankee pitcher is pitching a no-hitter," my father said. "A perfect game." My father was a casual fan, but this was obviously something special.

"Who's the pitcher?" I asked.

"Someone named Don Larsen," he recalled.

I knew the name, though it was hardly of the Ford-Turley-Maglie-Erskine-Newcombe variety, other pitchers in that 1956 Series.

When we began to drive, it was still in the relatively early stages of the game. As we drove, I noticed people on sidewalks stopping and standing to watch the game on televisions in windows in department and appliance stores. When we reached our destination, workers listened to the game on the radio.

I don't remember the announcer's details today—whether the shadows of the stadium roof had covered the mound, whether a breeze had picked up, whether the D train was rumbling in the distance. But I remember that when Dale Mitchell took a still controversial (was it high?) third strike called by the umpire Babe Pinelli to seal the perfect game, shouts erupted.

It seemed people were connected to this event, the only World Series perfect game, in a way they would probably not be today. The World Series seemed to tie the nation together in a way it no longer does. Late-night World Series games, and late-late-night World Series games, along with a sinking feeling about baseball, and the assault on the senses of so many other sports have dimmed and diminished what were once indelible moments.

Yesterday, Don Larsen, white-haired but, at 6'4", still looking fit at age 66, despite being involved in a 30-vehicle collision a few months ago on a California highway, came to town with his wife, Corrine, from their home in Hayden Lake, Idaho. Larsen participated in the Yankees' annual Old-Timers' Day, and of course that game of 40 years ago was recalled. In fact, he can hardly go anywhere without people bringing it up.

When Larsen was asked if he ever gets tired of talking about it, he replied, "Why should I?"

Larsen was 27 years old and still had wild streaks, on and off the field. In the second game of the Series, the Yankees provided him with a 6–0 lead, but he had control trouble in the second inning, gave up two runs, and manager Casey Stengel removed him from the game with two outs and the bases loaded.

"I wasn't mad at Casey," Larsen said. "I was mad at myself. And besides, when I think back on it, if I hadn't been taken out of the game I might not have had all the circumstances for the perfect game three days later."

But a year before, in his first spring training with the Yankees after having been traded to them from the Orioles, Larsen fell asleep at the wheel of his car and rammed into a telephone pole.

"I wasn't drinking," he said. "It was Sunday and the bars were closed in Florida. I was just goofin' off."

It was 4:00 in the morning. He went straight from the police station to the ballpark. When he told Stengel what had happened, the manager said, "Go to the outfield, out of the line of fire, and I'll handle the press."

Stengel began his explanation, "The pole jumped out into the road."

Larsen was an eye-popping 3–21 with Baltimore in 1954—the Orioles considered turning him into an outfielder—but he beat the Yankees in two of those games. The Yankees thought he had potential and dealt for him. He was 9–2 in 1955 and 11–5 in '56.

In the perfect game, he threw only 97 pitches. He encountered just a handful of problems. He had three balls on only one batter, Pee Wee Reese, in the first inning, and struck him out. Gil McDougald made a great play in the hole at shortstop to throw out Jackie Robinson at first base in the second inning. In the fifth, Gil Hodges flied deep to left-center field, but Mickey Mantle made a one-handed grab.

"Mickey wasn't the greatest fielder," Larsen said, "but he was so fast he could outrun almost anything.

"Other than that—and a long foul ball that Sandy Amoros hit—everything went very quickly. My control was just right there.

"I knew I had a no-hitter, but I didn't know I had a perfect game until I struck out Mitchell and Yogi Berra came running out and jumped on me. He almost knocked me over."

Larsen's salary was about $12,000 at the time. He was increased by about another $500 the next season. The most he ever made in baseball was $20,000 with Houston in 1965, near the end of his 14-season career.

He finished with an 81–91 record, and no other game he pitched came close to that perfect game. He sold insurance afterward, then sold paper for a company in San Jose, California, for 24 years.

Now he fishes for salmon in the Idaho rivers.

"I'm lucky," he said. "Lucky to still be alive so I can enjoy all this."

COME HOME, ALLIE REYNOLDS

August 29, 1988

THE MERE IDEA that Reggie Jackson would return for the last month of the season to play for the Yankees again in the team's supposed pennant drive made many shake their heads. After all, the main problem with the Yankees, as everyone knows, is not hitting, it's pitching.

The notion—perhaps spawned by Reggie, carried along by a lawyer friend, and receiving an allegedly "lukewarm" reception by George Steinbrenner—apparently was to bring back the glory days in a living embodiment of a storied, gloried pinstriper. If the Yankee brass in these dire times were to send out smoke signals to former Yankees, however, it should be to old hurlers, not to ancient sluggers.

Jackson, now 42 years old, retired last season as a member of the Oakland Athletics.

Some believe that Reginald Martinez Jackson had retired a few years before that but, what with the pressing demands of life in general, had simply neglected or forgotten to tell his employers. To many, Reggie is no longer Mr. October, but Mr. November.

But what if one of those old great Yankee pitchers could come back, and move into the starting rotation, or shore up the bullpen? Oh, what a dream! So calls were made to some of the best.

How's the old wing? How long would it take for them to get back in shape? Can they do it?

"Are you kidding?" asked Lefty Gomez, who had just come in to his house in Novato, California, from picking fruit off his fruit trees: two apple trees, a peach tree, a pear tree, two fig trees, an orange tree, a grapefruit tree, and a plum tree. "I'm nearly 80 years old, and I haven't pitched in the major leagues in 45 years." No way he could still pitch? "No way at all," he said. "Once a Yankee always a Yankee, but I can't throw the ball four feet. I'd love to help, but even though I'm left-handed, I still think it's a ridiculous idea."

Allie Reynolds, now 73 years old, and still in the "mud business"—he supplies oil-field service materials—answered a call in Oklahoma City. "I remember my second no-hitter in 1951," said Reynolds. "It was against the Red Sox at the end of September, and it kept us in the pennant race. We won it two days later. My arm still feels good, it's just that the ball doesn't go very far when I throw it. I'm up to 240 pounds, from my playing weight of 210. I don't move very fast anymore, but then, I don't have to."

But Allie, the Yankees are desperate for help on the mound. "I'm sorry," he said. "It's just not in the cards." Closer to Yankee Stadium, a man in Upstate New York, near Rochester, picked up a ringing telephone in his home. He had just come in from replanting garlic plants. "I feel great," said Vic Raschi, the former Springfield Rifle, now 69 years old. "I played recently in an old-timers' game in Minnesota. I cheated a little on the mound. I moved up two feet from the rubber. I threw, and the ball got to the plate, though I wasn't sure how long it would take before it did."

Raschi, who has a replacement hip, got the batter to ground out, and then left the game. "I didn't want to overdo it," he said.

But couldn't he be counted on for the stretch run this season? What a way to be remembered.

"Impossible," he said, with sadness in his voice. "Those garlic plants have worn me out." And Steady Eddie Lopat? "The arm's okay," said the 70-year-old Yankee scout, who lives in New Jersey. "But I'm afraid I could only throw up mortar lobs. As for my body, well, I weigh about the same as when I played, it's just that the sands have shifted."

Hmm, well, you could always count on Luis "Yo-Yo" Arroyo, anyway. He sauntered out of the bullpen and rarely failed to put out the fire. Arroyo, now 61, is a scout for the Yankees in the Caribbean.

"I had an elbow operation in 1964, which finished me," said Luis from his home in Penuelas, Puerto Rico, "and now, when I have to do a lot of writing of scouting reports, my arm gets tired, and I need someone to help me write them up. I couldn't fool people anymore with my pitching. I'm not that crazy to even try."

"How about me!" said Ryne Duren, from his home in Stoughton, Wisconsin. "I'm only 59, and my eyes are better than ever!" Duren wore thick, tinted glasses and, when he came in in relief and threw warm-up pitches that whizzed against the backstop, made hitters' knees shake. After the initial enthusiasm, he recalled pitching to college kids a few years ago, and waking the next morning with an arm throbbing with soreness. "I'm afraid I wouldn't be of much use," he said.

Catfish Hunter, from Hertford, North Carolina, took a few moments from his soybean, corn, and peanut crops to turn down a chance to return to the mound at Yankee Stadium. "They definitely need pitching, but they definitely don't need me," he said. "I'm afraid a line drive back to the box would kill me."

Jim "Bulldog" Bouton, who pitches semipro baseball in New Jersey, said, "No question I could still help the ballclub, but don't have George call me. I don't want him hassling me. Not now. I'm in the playoffs with the Teaneck Merchants, and that's all I have time for."

Sparky Lyle, also living in New Jersey, and a greeter in a casino in Atlantic City, was asked how his arm is.

"I don't know," he said, "and I don't wanna find out."

So, no luck. But calls were also out to Whitey Ford, Spec Shea, Bob Kuzava, Don Larsen, Dirt Tidrow, and sundry others.

Meanwhile, if Reggie returns to the Yankees, it should be as a pitcher. Or at least a pitching coach—the Yankees seemingly can never get enough of those, either.

NIEKRO: TRYING TO PITCH FOREVER

September 5, 1987

ABOUT A YEAR AGO, Ted Turner, the television mogul who has boats and a baseball team to play with, wondered about Phil Niekro, his former knuckleballing employee on the Atlanta Braves. Niekro was then seeking to hang on as a pitcher in the major leagues.

"When is he going to learn," said Turner, "that you can't pitch forever?" Personally, I wish he'd never learn. Niekro, or Knucksie, as he is known in diamond circles, is 48 years old, about nine months older than the sportswriter who is taking up space here. Niekro was the last major league ballplayer who is actually older than the writer.

We get older—the world around us gets older—marking time in various ways, and not simply by the calendar.

Trees do it by their rings, tigers by their teeth, and some of us one day look around and wonder how it is that cops have suddenly got so young.

Mark Twain saw it another way. He made rare visits back to Hannibal, Missouri, and in his last, at age 77, he returned to the house on Hill Street in which he was born. "It all seems so small to me," Twain said. "I suppose if I should come back here 10 years from now it would be the size of a birdhouse." For many Americans, time is marked, not necessarily by the shrinking of their old houses, but by the aging of their baseball heroes.

There was a time when the ballplayers all seemed so much older, men we once noticed standing outside of the clubhouse waiting for autographs after a game, who smoked cigarettes and wore bright sport coats and slicked back their hair.

Now if, as seems plausible, it is indeed the end of the road for Philip Henry Niekro, born on April Fool's Day, 1939, then all of the ballplayers, every single last tobacco-plug one of them, will be younger than the writer.

Last Monday night Knucksie was given his release by the Toronto Blue Jays, who only about a month before had purchased him from the Indians for the stretch drive.

Now Niekro, the white-haired hurler of 20 vintage years and four teams in the big leagues, has gone home to Linburg, Georgia, conceivably never again to float a baseball seriously in a ballgame. But it is the decision of others, not his.

When would Knucksie learn that you can't pitch forever? Well, after the Braves released him at age 44—and he had the second-best pitching record on the team—he went to the Yankees and won 32 games in two seasons.

His last victory for the Yankees, before they released him, was the final game of the 1985 season. He beat the Blue Jays 8–0 and did it with the utmost style. At age 46, he wanted to prove that his fastball could still win games. And so he stored the knuckleball that he had thrown almost exclusively for his entire professional career.

And he set the Blue Jays down inning after inning.

Niekro's brother, Joe, also a pitcher then on the Yankees, queried him about the knuckleball in the fifth inning. "When you gonna throw one?" he asked.

"Not even my brother believed I could do it," Phil Niekro recalled. "I just looked at him and laughed."

But Knucksie threw two knucklers, the last two pitches to the last batter of the game, Jeff Burroughs, and struck him out. "I just couldn't see pitching the most important game of my career without throwing one," he said. In 1986 Niekro was signed by the Indians, and had an 11–11 record with one of baseball's worst teams. This season he was 7–11 before being dealt to Toronto. He pitched three games there. "He did well in the first two," said Howard Starkman, the Toronto public relations director. "But he didn't win. And then the third game, last Saturday, Oakland bombed him for five runs in two-thirds of an inning."

Knucksie ached for a chance to get into a World Series, his first. He had been in two league championships series—both with Atlanta, in 1969 against the Mets and 1982 against the Cardinals—and his club lost in three straight both times. He had hoped for this chance with Toronto. It was not to be.

When Toronto got Mike Flanagan from the Orioles—they wanted another southpaw—they found their 48-year-old right-hander dispensable.

Niekro had said several years ago that it made him mad when he had lost five games in a row and people said he was finished. He complained that they don't say that about younger pitchers. "But with me, two losses in a row means curtain time," he said. Exactly. He was 0–2 with Toronto. In his autobiography, *Knuckle Balls*, published last year, Knucksie wrote that it also riled him that people kept asking him the same question, "When are you going to retire?"

"I don't know when I'm gonna retire, and nobody can convince me why a 47- or 48-year-old man can't continue to play baseball," he said. "Someone has to be the oldest player in the game, and I guess that I just have to be that person."

While he was still that person, in 1985, Niekro recalled being in the Yankee clubhouse on Old-Timers' Day. "When ya look in the players' eyes, as they see all their boyhood heroes appear before them, it looks like you're lookin' into the eyes of a 12-year-old," Niekro wrote. "I feel the same way. God, I feel like a 40-year-old again, bein' around these guys."

Now he's gone, and the writer wonders, what next? How will the world look and behave when he is older than every major leaguer striding the earth? After Knucksie, the deluge?

A YANKEE DINOSAUR CALLED RAGS

August 10, 1989

BEHIND THE LEFT-CENTER-FIELD fence in Yankee Stadium there is kept on the bullpen bench a dinosaur, in pinstripes. Depending on your sightline, he may be seen directly beyond one of the retired numbers on the row of painted baseballs on the fence, behind either No. 4 (Gehrig), 3 (Ruth), 5 (DiMaggio), 7 (Mantle), 37 (Stengel), a pair of 8s (Berra and Dickey), 16 (Ford), 15 (Munson), 32 (Howard), 9 (Maris), 10 (Rizzuto), or 1 (Martin).

There's another way to locate him. He's usually embosomed under the canopy and behind the water cooler, has been for years. If someone new wanders by and plops down in his spot, he is quickly shooed off.

"I guess you could say we're creatures of habit," said the dinosaur.

He is a left-handed dinosaur, wears a funny cap with a bill to keep the sun out of his eyes, and wears a uniform with a number of his own on the back, 19, which one day may find its way onto the outfield fence.

The dinosaur is called Rags. He is also known as David Allen Righetti, relief pitcher.

"I'm a dinosaur," he said recently, "but only by default. It's kind of an unfortunate thing. I wish there were more."

Rags Righetti seems a thing from out of prehistoric times, though, at age 31, he retains a boyish smile and a rugged (not to say scaly) competitor's fervor. He is the only player in uniform

(Dave Winfield has been out all season with a back injury) who was a member of a pennant-winning Yankee team. This was back at the dim turn of the decade, in 1981, a strike-torn season, but one that saw the Yankees land in the World Series. They lost to the Dodgers, though the principal owner of the team salvaged some glory by beating up two dastardly phantoms in a hotel elevator in Los Angeles.

"I was a rookie in 1981, and I sat quietly on the front of the bus or the plane or in the corner of the clubhouse and watched guys like Nettles and Reggie and Goose and Guidry," said Righetti. "There was such confidence I remember before the fifth and final game in the playoffs against Milwaukee, which had a very good team. We just knew we'd find a way to win. And we did."

But even then there were strange goings-on from above. "Before the playoffs, the pitchers were running in the outfield, and Goose sprained his ankle," said Righetti, about Gossage, the team's top reliever then. The owner, George Steinbrenner, issued an edict. "As I recall, the pitchers' running was restricted, and we were then sent to a little room to talk ball."

It was funny, he said, but it didn't matter. "The feeling was, no matter what, we'd win. It was expected. You know, coming up in the organization, everybody had a ring. All through the Yankee minor leagues. Not just the managers and coaches, but the players, too. I played on four minor league teams, and I won pennants on all of them. That was the Yankee tradition."

But the parent team wouldn't win again—or hasn't.

"I'm not sure what happened, but so many things changed," he said. "Sometimes I look back and think, if only we'd have kept one guy, either this guy or that, maybe, maybe.... We lost Goose after 1983, and I went from starter to reliever. I'm not sure that was the best thing for the team in the long run. I've always felt that the key to winning is the starting staff."

Righetti said the years have been frustrating ones, sometimes depressing ones. "But you keep hoping," he said. "Every day now, I drive to the ballpark and I'm pumped up. We're under .500 in the standings, but we're still in the race. Every game is important, incredible as that is.

"And I think, *Okay, let's just not lose this one in one of those crazy ways,* and if we can just get a winning streak going, and don't fall apart now. We have to stay in the race now because there are too many teams that we'd have to climb over in September, if we had to make our run then."

He's gone through pitching changes, from what he called his "pigheadedness"—trying to overpower most hitters—to more of a thinking-man's fireman.

The dinosaur has had his own good days and bad, and some of the fans in the stands even boo him when he enters a game. But he seeks to maintain his equilibrium, with the ballplayers' frequent remedy, gallows humor.

"Our bullpen is right under the bleachers, and we hear a lot of stuff from fans," said Righetti. "In the last two years, Charles Hudson would come out there and then hide behind a pillar, disguise his voice, and act like a fan. He'd ride us, give us the Bronx cheer, the whole works. Scott Nielsen went for a month thinking it was the real thing. I don't think Neil Allen ever found out."

Those pitchers, too, are now gone. But Rags the dinosaur remains, a remembering remnant of a time when champions roamed the Yankee Stadium earth.

THE FUTURE IS UNCLEAR
FOR HOWE

July 3, 1996

NOW IT IS OVER. Maybe. For in years past it has been an unrewarding exercise to try to write the end of the sad, the tragic, the remarkable—even, to be sure, the uplifting—Steve Howe story. Each time it has been done, Howe somehow finds a way to add a new chapter. Seven times Steve Howe has been suspended from baseball for substance abuse. Seven times he came back—perhaps some kind of perverse record in itself. But now, well, maybe now the baseball book is closed on his career.

Eleven days ago, the 38-year-old left-handed relief pitcher was released from the Yankees, a team he had pitched for without much off-field incident for the last six years. He wasn't getting batters out, especially left-handed batters, who were hitting a gaudy .333 against his offerings. When Joe McIlvaine, the Mets' general manager, was asked if he would pursue Howe, he said, "I can tell you unequivocally, no. We have no interest in Steve Howe. Can I make it any clearer? The man's had seven chances. There's no way I'll take that on."

Some teams did call Howe's agent, Dick Moss. And one, San Francisco, agreed to give him a look. And then backed out when Howe was arrested two days after his release.

While Howe was preparing to board a plane at Kennedy Airport, a loaded .357 Magnum was found in his luggage, according to the Port Authority police. He said it belonged to his wife, Cindy. She said that she had packed the gun, which she uses for protection when he is on the road, and that in the rush she hadn't realized it was loaded. The couple, with their two young children, were headed back to their home in Whitefish, Montana, where Howe is a hunter and carries a weapon in his pickup truck. He was arraigned in Queens criminal court and freed on his own recognizance. He will have to return next week to answer charges of criminal possession of a weapon.

"We were at the counter declaring the weapon when all this happened," Howe said.

Perhaps. Howe has often had excuses for his behavior, and for what has mostly got him in trouble in the past, his drug addiction. Once, as a member of the Dodgers, he said he wanted to play for Minnesota and get away from the "drug culture" of Los Angeles. But that same culture seemed to follow him wherever he went— including Minnesota and Montana. But for the last seven years, he said, "I've been clean."

Indeed, he has submitted to a urine analysis every other day for that period. And he has never failed. And after a relatively poor season last year he was not on the spring training roster, but George Steinbrenner, the Yankee principal owner, succumbed to Howe's appeal for another chance, calling the pitcher, in light of his struggles, "a worthy young man."

In 25 appearances this season, Howe was 0–1, with just one save and a 6.35 earned-run average. But he could still throw a fastball at 92 mph, though Joe Torre, the Yankee manager, said he had lost the hop that had stymied hitters for a good portion of Howe's 12-year big-league career. That career included being voted National League Rookie of the Year in 1980, a World Series victory, and an All-Star Game appearance while with the Dodgers.

"After the gun incident," Bob Quinn, general manager of the Giants, said yesterday, "we decided not to go ahead with signing him." It was obvious that the Giants, like other teams, did not want to deal with the criticisms that would follow.

"It looks like his baseball career is over," said Moss, Howe's agent.

Before his release, Howe had talked about staying clean. He said Dwight Gooden, coming off two drug suspensions, had approached him when he joined the Yankees this season and asked how Howe was able to stay clean.

"I told Doc, 'You can't let success go to your head, and you will have to deal with adversity in the same way,'" Howe recalled. "Every day is a challenge. There are no easy days for a drug addict. People look at you and say, 'You're a major league ballplayer. You have money, fame, good times.' But what's wrong with this picture? You have to try to control your urges. And we should be used to trying to control ourselves. We made it up here. And by ourselves. Nobody gave us nothing. It's just not easy."

Howe has had great support from friends and family, especially Cindy. But now in Montana he seemingly begins life without baseball. There will be no structure supplied by baseball for drug testing, no incentives for fame and fortune.

What now, Steve Howe?

ANTICIPATION AND DRAMA
AT STADIUM

July 11, 1997

THE DRAMA WAS BUILDING. If this were a novel, it might begin with it being a dark and stormy night; if a play, a roll of thunder as the curtain rises. But sometimes reality snuffs invention, and last evening was a night of surpassing loveliness, with a sweet scent of summer in the air at Yankee Stadium. But, also, with an unmistakable sense of electricity.

"Everybody," Paul O'Neill, the Yankee outfielder, was saying from his stool in the clubhouse yesterday before the contest against the Motown Ten, "everybody is excited. I mean, players are fans, they're just like other people. They're curious to see what all this is about."

"We're all anxious to see him pitch," said Don Zimmer, the Yankee coach, who has spent half a century in professional baseball. "I don't ever remember this kind of anticipation for one player. I remember when I was with the Dodgers and Sandy Koufax came up, and he was so wild that the regulars didn't want to face him in batting practice. He couldn't throw the ball into the cage. That was awesome, too, but in a different way from this."

"There's such a mystique built up," said David Cone, the Yankees' All-Star hurler, with a gleam in his eye. "I mean, a guy who throws a fastball 100 miles an hour, a forkball at 90, with pinpoint control. I'll sneak into the clubhouse to watch on television—better to see how his ball moves."

Someone asked if anyone had seen him yet—the him being, of course, Hideki Irabu, the 28-year-old right-handed pitcher, who has been the subject of headlines for six weeks. Or ever since George Steinbrenner finally wrested him from the San Diego Padres—who had original American rights to him—and Japan, which had his birthright, as well as, it assumed, his earthly rights.

It was the Yankees, Irabu said, or nothing—nothing, presumably, being a return to Chiba, his hometown, and cooling it. And now he had swept through a few warm-up weeks of Class A, Double A, and Triple A ball, and had reached his dream—pitching in Yankee *pinsutoraipu* (in other words, pinstripes.)

"I just met him for the first time when he came into the clubhouse," said Cone. "He said, 'Nice to meet you'—in perfect English." And? "And I said, 'Welcome.' I said, 'If there's anything I could do to help, I'd be happy to.' He said, 'Thank you.' Nothing else. That might be the extent of his English."

Some Yankees had grumbled earlier about the ink and money and position this highest-paid rookie in baseball history was getting—$12.8 million over four years. For the most part, though, much of that was past.

Doc Gooden, who had some concerns at one point that Irabu might be taking his spot in the starting rotation, seemed to be taking the new arrival in some stride. Gooden, with interleague play on his mind, asked with a smile, "Can you hit?"

"He laughed," recalled Gooden, "and said, 'No.'"

What would the major leaguers be watching for? "Nervousness," Gooden said. "I mean, a different country, all the hype, New York City—and the Yankees."

"Competitiveness," Cone said. "How he will react when runners are on base. And what he does when he gets ahead of a hitter—can he bury him?"

Sitting alone in front of a corner locker in the Yankee clubhouse was a stocky, dark-haired man quietly tying on a pair of size 12 baseball shoes. He seemed oblivious to the hurly-burly. But the name plate above the locker told the tale simply. It read: "IRABU."

To a standing ovation, Irabu went to the mound to start the game. He quickly dispatched the first three batters to face him, striking out two. The near-capacity crowd of 51,000 and change was itchy with excitement. There were at least nine K-corners in the stands recording his whiffs.

Irabu, with a soupçon of a double chin and wicked stuff, went on to hurl six and two-thirds innings, giving up two runs on five hits and four walks, with nine strikeouts. On a great play by third baseman Charlie Hayes to end an inning, he tipped his cap, demonstrating a universal language for admiration. When manager Joe Torre removed him with two outs and none on in the seventh and a 10–2 lead, the crowd stood again and cheered their new hero, some bowing low.

Irabu disappeared into the dugout, but then, by acclaim, reemerged for a cap-waving encore. The crowd went bananas.

Clearly, he has found a snug home in the Bronx.

PETTITTE: THE TRADE NEVER MADE STILL GOLDEN

Thursday, October 5, 2000

OAKLAND, CALIFORNIA — It was right at the trading deadline, at the end of July of last year, and the news had leaked. The Yankees were about to deal one of their top pitchers. Andy Pettitte, who had been struggling, was about to change uniforms, swapping the Bronx Bomber pinstripes for the Phillies' candy stripes.

"It was ready to happen, if the Boss wanted it," recalled Brian Cashman, the Yankees' general manager. The Boss was one George Michael Steinbrenner III. "But almost everyone in the organization wanted Andy to stay, especially me," Cashman said. "I'm a big believer in a track record, and Andy had a great track record with us. George listened—that's one of his virtues—and decided not to pull the trigger."

When the trade wasn't made, Pettitte called Cashman aside in the clubhouse.

"Thanks for keeping me here," Pettitte said.

Cashman held up his hand, with his 1998 Yankee World Series ring glistening.

"I wouldn't have this without you," Cashman said.

Last night, the Yankees once again were returning the thank you to Pettitte, who was masterly in beating the A's 4–0 to tie the series at one game apiece as the show journeys across the continent to resume tomorrow at Yankee Stadium.

When the Yankees had become desperate for a victory, had become almost despairing for a victory—they had lost 16 of their last 19 games, and eight straight, including Game 1 of this series on Tuesday—Andrew Eugene Pettitte of Baton Rouge, Louisiana, a left-hander, came to the rescue, all 6′5″, 225 pounds of him.

In fact, in his last start, in the last weekend of the regular season, Pettitte, going for his 20th victory in a game against Baltimore, lasted just one and a third innings; he was pounded for nine runs and was also on the mound long enough to walk three straight batters, an anomaly with a control pitcher like Pettitte.

"It's a whole new season," Pettitte had said before this series began. "The postseason is different. You can throw out the end of the season."

The opposition seemed to agree. "He's the pitcher on the Yankees who scares us the most," A's third baseman Eric Chavez said.

"He's a big-game pitcher," said Randy Velarde, the A's second baseman. "He's made for this kind of atmosphere."

And their manager, Art Howe, said, "Pettitte won't wilt, he's not going to beat himself. You've got to beat him."

Last night Pettitte, 7–4 in postseason play, was the picture of professionalism. Watching his intensity on the mound, it was clear that he understood he had to be this good since the Yankees' bats appeared to be made of sponge. He even was seen to be mumbling to himself. "He holds little conferences with himself on the mound," Joe Torre, the Yankee manager, said.

What does he say? "If I start overthrowing, I'll say something like, 'Stay back,'" Pettitte said. "It's just to get me locked in my concentration, and my focus tonight was good." At one point in the middle of the game, Pettitte retired 13 straight batters. This is not a new thing. At age 28, and over the last five years, he trails only Pedro Martinez and Greg Maddux in total wins—Pettitte has 88, two behind Martinez and Maddux. Then the Yankees scored three runs in the sixth. This was a surfeit of riches, since last night Pettitte needed but one run to achieve his goal.

Pettitte put out just a few small Oakland uprisings, until the eighth. Then, with two out, he gave up a double to Ramon Hernandez. An easy ground ball by Terrence Long to Luis Sojo at second was going to get him out of the inning, but Sojo tripped himself, and flipped into the air and fell in a heap, like a vaudeville routine, still holding the ball. With runners now on first and third, and Pettitte having thrown 100 pitches and some change, Torre decided that Pettitte had done more than his share for the evening. He removed him for the relief pitcher Mariano Rivera, who retired the next batter and shut the A's down in the ninth.

Pettitte looked stunned when he was removed. "I thought, *This ain't gonna happen*," he said. "This was a huge game for us. I didn't want to come out." But then he righted himself and left the game graciously. Which is of a piece with what we know about Pettitte. "He's the kind of guy who doesn't call attention to himself," Cashman had said. "He's such a quiet, decent person."

Cashman thought back about that time in July of 1999 when Pettitte almost became a Phillies pitcher.

"But from that point forward," Cashman recalled, "he went 6–1. It was lights out."

Like, if you're keeping score, last night.

GOODEN: CONQUERING MORE THAN THE STRIKE ZONE

July 11, 1996

THERE WAS TROUBLE with Dwight Gooden. Mel Stottlemyre popped out of the Yankee dugout and made his way to the mound to talk to the tall, sweating pitcher as the Brewers threatened in the fifth inning of a game last week.

Stottlemyre is the Yankee pitching coach and was the Mets' pitching coach when Gooden was the toast of the baseball world, considered at age 19 the next greatest, hardest-throwing pitcher since Walter Johnson, or at least Tom Seaver.

That was before Gooden's shoulder surgery, before his drug and alcohol problems, before his two suspensions from baseball, before, as Gooden admits now, he embarked on a dark, dangerous, and reckless life.

Stottlemyre knew Gooden's arm was a little tired last week, and before the Milwaukee game he even suggested that the pitcher might like another day's rest. "No," said Gooden, "I've waited too long for this."

That is, waited too long to be in the regular rotation, or any rotation, for that matter. His last suspension was for a year and a half, and he spent last summer not in big-league double knits but coaching his son's Little League team in Tampa, Florida, wondering if he would ever get another shot at pitching in the majors.

The Yanks were leading 5–1, with two outs in the fifth, when Stottlemyre approached the mound at Yankee Stadium. Gooden had walked the previous batter on four pitches, and now there were runners on first and second. The cleanup man, Greg Vaughn, was up.

"Don't overthrow," Stottlemyre told Gooden. "Let nature take its course. Think more location."

Stottlemyre left. Gooden's next two pitches were sliders, and Vaughn flied to left on the second one to end the inning.

It preserved the lead and helped preserve a victory that increased the Yankees' lead over Baltimore in the American League East. It also gave Gooden his eighth straight victory against four losses.

"This was as good an indication of Doc Gooden today as anything else," said Stottlemyre. "In times past, Gooden would have tried to overpower the hitter, to overthrow. Once he could do it. Now he's a little older and has to be a little wiser. And he is. He can still throw the ball in the 90-mile-per-hour range, but it's the low 90s and not the high 90s as when he was younger. And he didn't throw any fastballs to Vaughn but gave him sliders on the corners."

With David Cone out and Jimmy Key belatedly regaining his form, Gooden has now joined Andy Pettitte as one of the unexpected aces of the staff. He has streamlined his pitching motion with a shorter leg kick and a quicker release. The result has been fewer chances to make mistakes and sharper control. His most extraordinary performance was the no-hitter he threw May 14 against Seattle at the Stadium. His next start will come tomorrow when the Yankees face the Orioles at Camden Yards.

Gooden's growth has not been restricted to baseball. He has seen what is needed to make his life whole, and he has taken those steps.

And like Darryl Strawberry, Gooden's former and current teammate whose career rose and fell in similar fashion, Gooden came to the Yankees with the idea that this could well be his last chance.

Gooden was determined not to blow it by being anything but hard working and grateful for the opportunity.

When Gooden saw Strawberry, who returned to the Yankees last Sunday, come into the clubhouse, they embraced. The trouble each has brought on himself the last few years has, apparently, given each a sense of humility.

Stottlemyre remembers when Dwight Gooden first appeared in the Yankees' spring training camp. "He was like a rookie," said the Yankee pitching coach. "He seemed so excited to be there. He came early and stayed late. And did everything we asked, and eagerly."

"What I see in Doc now," said David Cone, the Yankee pitcher, who had also been a teammate with the Mets, "is a sparkle in his eye. I hadn't realized it wasn't there until I saw it this spring. And it hasn't gone away."

His muscled right arm still moist from a rubdown in the trainer's room, Gooden sat in front of his locker recently and explained the difference this way: "I appreciate what I have now. And I understand how much I nearly lost."

He remembers driving at night into the drug neighborhoods of Tampa and getting his fixes. "I could've been killed," he said. He had talked about suicide, and at one point about putting a gun to his head.

"And when I was suspended the first time," he said, "I went to my parents to tell them. I was really worried. I said, 'I have bad news, and I have good news. The bad news is, I've been suspended from baseball. The good news is, I'm sick and I'm going to get help.' I remember my mom crying, and my father said nothing. The disappointment in his eyes was so obvious. That was just terrible for me."

Gooden was admitted to Smithers Institute in Manhattan in 1987 for 30 days in rehabilitation and then the Betty Ford Center for another rehab in 1994.

He says that come September he will have been clean of drugs for two years and that he is tested three times a week by Major League Baseball. Gooden's rise and fall and rise again is the stuff of movies, apparently, because he has received an offer to make his life story into a film. "I want to do it because I want kids to see how you can ruin your life, even one when you're pretty much on top of the world," said Gooden.

When he came to the Yankees, he approached Steve Howe, the recently released relief pitcher, about the way to stay clean. Howe had been suspended seven times from baseball for substance abuse, and seven times made comebacks.

"I used to sit in the back of the bus with Dwight and Howe and heard the conversations," said Cone. "I remember Howe saying how difficult it is when you're a drug addict. But that to stay away you have to have help. Have people to talk to."

Gooden has. "You have to go to meetings, and it has been very important for me to have a sponsor," he said. A sponsor must be someone else recovering from substance abuse, and Gooden's is a man named Ron Dock, who lives in Tampa.

"For me," said Gooden, "the worst time is during holidays. People tend to drink during those periods. And I did. And it was the drinking that let down my defenses and led to my drug use. So I know I have to stay away from drinking. And last New Year's Eve, I went over to my sister's house, and a lot of my family was there, and they were drinking. I got the urge. And instead of going to the bottle, I called Ron. He said, 'You can drink, and throw away the rest of your life,' or you can just leave the house and control your life. I needed to talk to him. I left the house."

But it was Howe who told Gooden that one of the worst times for a recovering substance abuser was when things were going either very well, or very poorly. "At those times," said Gooden, "you feel you can either do anything you want and nothing can happen to you, or you don't care what happens to you, that it can't be as bad as that moment."

Gooden began the season with four straight losses and was on the verge of either going to the bullpen or being sent to the minor leagues. But he kept his head and kept trying to pitch to spots instead of "maxing out," as he called his fastball that is thrown as hard as possible, and anywhere, as long as it's over the plate. "But that's being a thrower and not a pitcher," he said.

And in some ways, that is the difference, for Gooden, in being a responsible adult. "Some people have said Dwight's been a lucky pitcher because he has won games with a fairly high earned-run average," said Stottlemyre. (Gooden's ERA is 4.20.) "But what I see is his ability to pitch out of jams. A few years ago, he would not have done that. A few years ago, the Brewers would have got to him in the fifth inning the other day."

Gooden seems more open than he ever has, more willing to confront his problems, more willing to talk of his responsibility to his family, particularly his wife, Monica, and Gooden's four children, three with Monica.

"The thing I've learned most of all," he said, "is that baseball comes third in my life. First comes the Highest Power, then my family, and then baseball. It's a matter of priorities. Once baseball was the most important thing, and my idea of me as a baseball player. I still love baseball, and I want very much to stay in the game. But now I believe I'd be okay without it. I wasn't sure before that I ever would. I've found now that my life is way more important than baseball."

CLEMENS: CHIN MUSIC

July 12, 2000

GEORGE STEINBRENNER, who is to baseball what Matthew Brady, Edward Steichen, and Richard Avedon are to photography, is an expert on focus.

This is what the Yankees' principal owner said Monday in regard to the Mets' charge after their weekend series that Roger Clemens purposely hit Mike Piazza in the head with a 92 mph fastball, and, to a markedly lesser degree, the protested interference call against Met first baseman Todd Zeile.

"They had to take the focus off the fact that they got their fannies handed to them this time," Steinbrenner said. "I'm not sure it wasn't a very wise public relations move for them to take the focus off the way they were beaten.

"I think Bobby Valentine and his people would love to take the focus off that, and have the people forget about the results."

What Steinbrenner—we can just picture him under a black cloth and behind that old boxy camera—is really doing is seeking to return the focus to where he believes the focus has suddenly become unfocused. That is, on his Bronx Bombers. But his defense of his pitcher, while understandable, is tasteless, if not reprehensible.

It is undeniable, of course, that the Yankees beat the Mets three out of four games last weekend, and four out of six in the Subway Series this year. And forget for a moment that an opposing player could very well have been killed, or severely maimed for life by a pitcher whose salary Steinbrenner pays.

The Clemens pitch, which produced a concussion in Piazza despite his wearing a plastic helmet for protection, is another matter. It's a well-worn axiom, as Steinbrenner adds, that fastball pitchers "have to live on the inside." And brushbacks are a century-old part of baseball. But that doesn't make it right. Steinbrenner said, "I know Roger, I know he's a family guy who loves his kids, and there's no way a future Hall of Famer like him is going to try to hurt somebody."

Maybe not. But Clemens is famous for hitting people, and is a virtuoso at "chin music." I remember talking to Seattle players a few years ago who said that Clemens hits every Mariner rookie the first time he sees him—"to send a message." A message that can be perilous.

I will never forget Tony Conigliaro of the Red Sox being hit in the face in 1967 with a fastball thrown by Jack Hamilton, who had a reputation like Clemens'. Conigliaro was a 22-year-old slugger, and on his way to a wonderful career. People at the game recall with horror the sound of Hamilton's fastball cracking into his face, like the smashing of a melon.

Tony C. was out for the remainder of that season, and the entire 1968 season. He returned to the game, but his eyesight was impaired, his head forever different from before. He retired in 1975, suffered a heart attack in 1982, and died in 1990 at age 45.

And Clemens' message to Piazza, on a night when his control was superb: you must pay for going 7-for-12 against me lifetime, with three homers.

Pitching inside is one thing. Head-hunting is another. Baseball should no longer tolerate that murderous tradition. And George Steinbrenner, sometimes, yes, a leader in positive ways in baseball, could have judiciously led here, too. But his focus in this grave case was not only self-serving, it was shamelessly distorted.

WELLS: COLORFUL PITCHER,
BUT NOT A STAND-UP GUY

March 3, 2003

WHAT IS A WIMP? A wimp, it says here, is a guy who acts tough but backs down when things actually get tough, or, in some cases, just prove embarrassing for him. A wimp is someone who won't stand up for what he says he believes, even if he believes what he has said.

A wimp is someone who blames others when he should be taking responsibility for his actions or statements, but then ducks from being accountable.

If David Wells is not a wimp, he has certainly been acting like one.

Wells is a big, beefy pitcher for the Yankees who wears the mantle of that great misnomer "sports hero," as most major professional athletes often do. And Wells in particular also enjoys a reputation, some of it self-proclaimed, of being a roughneck, a guy who is comfortable in a tumult, or just a bar fight. He rides a hog, can swiftly swig a six-pack, and favors heavy metal music.

His nickname is Boomer, presumably for the racket he makes. Now Boomer is also a spanking-new author. He has written a book that is due out March 14 that may never be confused with, say, *War and Peace* or *Wuthering Heights*, but it's a book with a more provocative title—including a hyperbolic exclamation point—*Perfect I'm Not! Boomer on Beer, Brawls, Backaches, and Baseball.*

Like a lot of the literati who also dabble as athletes, Wells did not sit down, quill pen in fist, and compose his opus. He spoke with a person named Chris Kreski, who wrote the book by taping and transcribing Wells' pearls of wisdom and then weaving together Wells' meditations and ruminations in grammatical form, with paragraphs and chapters and like niceties.

And true to his word in the title, anyway, Perfect Boomer Isn't!

Suddenly Boomer has found himself in the eye of a bookish storm, and he has run for cover.

For one thing, he espoused in the galleys released before the book that he was "half-drunk" when he pitched his perfect game for the Yankees in 1998. When Yankee management brought it to Wells' attention that this was disgraceful conduct for a man of the Yankee cloth—forget the tippling of the likes of Babe Ruth and Mickey Mantle—Boomer quailed. He changed his tune to say he had a headache.

In the galleys, Wells throws out a figure that 25 to 40 percent of current big leaguers use steroids. That's a pretty broad brush he paints with, and if he is going to do that, he should name names. He also takes shots at tendencies of some teammates, including Roger Clemens, Mike Mussina, and Andy Pettitte.

But then Boomer charged that the news media was distorting what was in the book.

But it is in the book, in black and white, no less.

At this point, Boomer spins around and becomes a stand-up guy. "It's my fault for not going through it with a fine-tooth comb," he said. Fine-tooth comb? He knew what he was saying when he said it. Or, when he was talking to Kreski, did he have a, well, headache? Even if he did, there were surely moments of lucidity when he could have applied whiteout. He obviously felt it was unnecessary, until the storm broke.

Wells has apologized to his manager, Joe Torre, and to his general manager, Brian Cashman. Apologize for what, telling the truth or just being lamebrained? Tolstoy and Emily Brontë never apologized for the contents of their literary output. This, though, puts Wells in the same category as Charles Barkley. When his book *Outrageous!* was released, Barkley, a famous prattler, discovered that he couldn't take the heat, either, and famously announced that he had been misquoted. In his own autobiography yet!

But Jim Bouton, the former Yankee pitcher, did not back down. When he wrote the revolutionary *Ball Four* with Leonard Schecter, he described, among other things, some unseemly pleasures of ballplayers. Bowie Kuhn, then baseball commissioner, called Bouton to his office. He wanted Bouton to sign a statement apologizing to the baseball community. Bouton read the statement and said, "I'm not signing this." And he didn't.

Bouton takes no credit for standing erect. "I wrote something, it was true, and I was going to stand by it," he said yesterday from his home in the Berkshires.

In regard to heroes, Bouton says there are two kinds. "There are the performers that people too often call courageous, when you go to the plate limping from an injury and produce with the bases loaded and the game on the line," he said. "But that's great athleticism. Then there's the other kind of courage, the kind that I find that's really courageous. And that's doing the right thing under certain pressures.

"It's a courage that goes beyond the foul lines. Muhammad Ali and Arthur Ashe, to name two, fit that description for me. Of course, after 9/11 especially, with policemen and firemen running up burning buildings to try to save people, we have to think again about what 'hero' or 'courage' really is."

In the end, Wells has demonstrated that he is less than courageous outside the foul lines, brawls and beer-swilling notwithstanding. But if he pitches well, all will be forgiven by fans and teammates—which is the nature of our world of sports.

One other thing: what about that photo in the book of Boomer standing naked in a field of sheep?

I truly hope he doesn't come out and say it was trick photography.

ABBOTT'S INSPIRATIONAL RETURN

May 21, 1999

SOME PEOPLE MAY surely be surprised to see Jim Abbott back on a major league mound, after what happened last year, or the year before, and, to be sure, the year before that. Even the first part of this season.

But Jim Abbott has always been full of surprises, including making the major leagues at all, the only pitcher known to have reached the big time with just one hand.

Yet here was the 6′3″, 210-pound left-hander for the Milwaukee Brewers getting ready to face the Mets' lineup in the first game of a doubleheader at Shea Stadium yesterday, with a dispiriting 0–4 record and lugging around an 8.49 earned-run average.

This was his first start in three weeks, after having been relegated to the bullpen after three unimpressive starts. He didn't complain of the demotion to manager Phil Garner. "How could I?" Abbott said. "I didn't have a leg to stand on."

Garner was sorry to drop the invariably polite, diligent Abbott from the rotation. "You hope he finds himself," Garner said. "He's a gutsy guy, and maybe the harder he tries the less effective he is. He's no longer a power pitcher, but more of a finesse pitcher, and he's in the transition of trying to master it. I just want him to throw free and easy."

Garner is giving him another shot as a starter, and Abbott knows he either succeeds now, or may very soon run out the string here.

Abbott has had some wonderful accomplishments in his 10 big-league seasons, including an 18–11 year with the Angels in 1991 and a no-hitter for the Yankees in 1993. But he fell on rocky times in Gotham and was traded to the Angels. Three seasons ago he won two games and lost 18, and was released by Anaheim. "I felt," he said, "uneasy with myself."

And he quit the game, at 29. He had rarely quit at anything, always determined to forge ahead. When he was five years old, in Flint, Michigan, his parents had fitted him with a hook for a hand. He came back from kindergarten crying that the other kids had made fun of him and were afraid to play with him. He removed the hook, never to wear it again.

He endeavored to prove himself in myriad ways, none more dramatically than on the athletic field, becoming a baseball star at he University of Michigan and going straight into the major leagues.

He inevitably became a hero and model to many who felt dis-advantaged.

"I don't carry that as a burden," he said. "I've looked at my life as a personal journey. But I'd say in 50 percent of the parks we play in, parents of kids with one hand, or some other disability, bring their kids to meet me."

And sometimes, as he did in Pittsburgh recently, he will play catch with them on the sidelines, removing their gloves to throw.

"It's the quietest kids that move me the most," he recalled. "You see their shyness, that they want to be like everybody else. I under-stand that. And they open up a little bit. It's inspiring."

After he quit baseball, he sat around his home in Michigan watching baseball games on television—he was still being paid around $3 million from his Angels contract—and realizing that it was still very much in his blood. After that season of inactivity, his agent called the White Sox, and Abbott last season returned to, of all places, Hickory, North Carolina, Class A ball.

He was moved up to Double A, then Triple A, and finally last September to the White Sox, for whom he was a remarkable 5–0 in that last month of the season. He became a free agent and signed a one-year contract with Milwaukee for $400,000 plus bonuses.

The game yesterday began forlornly for Abbott, and ended that way. Robin Ventura belted a bases-loaded home run off him in the first inning. His throwing error in the fourth cost him a run. In the bottom of the fifth, he gave up two hits with one out, and Garner removed him. The next batter homered, and Abbott, who was credited with giving up seven runs on seven hits in four and one-third innings and was the losing pitcher, could hardly have been a bundle of joy as he soaped himself in the shower, and contemplated his future, at 0–5.

"He obviously didn't do very well today," Garner said. "But right now he's still in the rotation."

In spring training, when Abbott was throwing well and looking like a star again, and hitting a single and laying down a sacrifice bunt, since National League pitchers must bat, Mark McGwire said it best.

"If Jim Abbott doesn't inspire you," McGwire said, "there's something wrong with you."

Nothing, really, has changed.

WAITE HOYT IN THE RAIN

August 28, 1984

ON SATURDAY, the Brooklyn Schoolboy died. Waite Charles Hoyt was just two weeks shy of his 85th birthday, but during his 21-year major league career and for much of his life, the Hall of Fame pitcher bore that fledgling's nickname.

It derived from his being signed to a contract with the New York Giants in 1915, when he was a 15-year-old student at Erasmus Hall High School in Brooklyn, though he didn't get into a big-league game with the Giants until 1918, and then for just one inning. The next year he was traded to the Boston Red Sox, and there his outstanding career took flight.

Though he pitched for seven clubs, his finest days were with the powerful Yankee teams from 1921 to 1930. Two years ago he was in New York from Cincinnati to attend a Yankee Old-Timers' Day, and the next week this reporter interviewed him for a television documentary.

"Years have flown," he said, "years have flown. The other day, when they called our names at the Stadium, I went out and stood on the mound just to see how it felt, once more. Oh, Jesus, it made you—well, I got teary, just standing there, oh, gee, did I."

He was a man of what might be average size today—6' and 180 pounds—but fairly large for his day. He was an old man now, white hair combed neatly straight back, tie just right, and sparkle in his eyes. They had obviously never lost the effervescence of his school days. That, and his large, strong hands, with which he punctuated, prodded, and shaped his sentences, were memorable.

Hoyt's big-league playing days ended in 1938, and four years later he became a radio announcer for the Cincinnati Reds games. His reputation as a raconteur grew. Fans looked forward to rain delays so they could listen to the stories he spun, the best of which were captured in a record album called *Waite Hoyt in the Rain*.

His favorites were about his teammate Babe Ruth. His tales of that grand American folk hero helped to illuminate not only Ruth but Waite Hoyt, as well.

"The first time that I ever saw Babe Ruth was in the Boston Red Sox clubhouse," he once said. "I walked in to report to the Red Sox, and they took me around and introduced me to everybody on the team, and when they got to him—you know, he couldn't remember anybody's name, he'd call you 'Happy Jack,' 'Pete,' 'Charlie,' 'Stud,' anything that came up in his mind—and he said, 'Hello, keed.' And he's sitting there, and he didn't look like a monster or anything, but he had black curly hair that dripped down over his forehead like ink, like there was spilled ink on his forehead, and he was utterly unbelievable.

"There is nothing like Ruth ever existed in this game of baseball. I remember we were playing the White Sox in Boston in 1919, and he hit a home run off Lefty Williams over the left-field fence in the ninth inning and won the game. It was majestic. It soared. We watched it and wondered, 'How can a guy hit a ball like that?' It was to the opposite field and off a left-handed pitcher, and it was an incredible feat. That was the dead-ball days, remember; the ball normally didn't carry. We were playing a doubleheader, and that was the first game, and the White Sox did not go into the clubhouse between games. They stood out there and sat on our bench and talked about the magnificence of that home run."

Ruth was a man of prodigious appetites, including drink, though "he was not a drunk," Hoyt emphasized. "And he liked the ladies, as who doesn't, but he liked them to an excess; he was a champion in that sport, too. But he was popular with everybody, and everybody forgave him. In Chicago, we used to go to church with Ruth. I'm Protestant, and he was Catholic, and the Protestants wanted to go with Ruth to watch him. And when the fella came for the contribution, why, Babe would put a $50 bill in the plate, and the guy's eyes would pop open. The Babe was paying for his sins, and we always got a kick out of that."

Another time in Chicago, an attractive "bon ton" woman was walking down the steps of the hotel where the Yankees were staying. Ruth and a group of teammates were about to take a taxi to the ballpark.

"The girl said to Babe, 'You're Mr. Ruth, aren't you?' He said, 'Yeah, that's me.' She said, 'Mr. Ruth, we're going to the ballpark. Would you like to ride with us?' He said, 'Gee, swell.' So he's waiting for the car, and finally two little old ladies join the girl and Ruth, and drive off. The car was one of those old electric things without a steering wheel! It's going about eight miles an hour. Ruth is in the back seat, and we pass him on Michigan Boulevard. We called out, 'Ho, Babe! Hello, Babe!' Babe looked kind of ugly in that big moon face, and he had an expression that would have killed a mule."

In 1948, when Ruth was dying of cancer, Hoyt and his wife were moved by a visit to the old slugger in his Manhattan hotel. The visit, which Bob Creamer described in the book *Babe*, was short, because Ruth was tired and in great pain. But before the Hoyts left, Ruth stood up and went to the refrigerator. He took a small vase with an orchid in it and brought it back to the living room. "Here," he said to Mrs. Hoyt, "I never gave you anything." Shortly afterward, in August 1948, Hoyt was one of the honorary pallbearers at Ruth's funeral.

"For some reason," said Hoyt, "there was a reverence connected with the funeral, a reverence, an amazement, a joke, everything that could possibly be incorporated in a man's character and disposition and personality. Joe Dugan, who was my roommate on the Yankees, was an honorary pallbearer, too. He was standing next to me as they were carrying the Babe down the steps of St. Pat's Cathedral here in New York. There must have been 5,000 people standing around on the sides of the street, and it was tremendous.

"It was a hot day, oh, a sinful day, about 98 degrees, and St. Pat's didn't have air-conditioning, and the sweat was running down our faces and dripping down our chins. And just as they were carrying the Babe down the steps of St. Pat's, Dugan, who used to talk out of the side of his mouth, whispered to me, 'Gee, I'd like to have a beer.' Just then the casket with the professional pallbearers went by. 'Well,' I said, 'so would the Babe.'"

BOUTON AND THE WRITE STUFF

December 10, 1983

THE PUBLICATION IN 1970 of Jim Bouton's *Ball Four*, a pica-resque, best-selling account of baseball life, resulted, he said, in the baseball establishment's branding him a Judas and a Benedict Arnold. Now Jim Bouton is on the ballot for election to the Baseball Hall of Fame.

"I am?" said Bouton, upon hearing this. "Are you sure?"

It's true. The ballots were mailed recently to veteran baseball writers. At Bouton's business office in Teaneck, New Jersey, yesterday, he was shown one, which included his name with 28 others, and was handed the supplemental material.

"Hmm, I barely made the statistics page," he said, looking it over. "I'd be quite surprised if I made it on the first ballot." He hardly cracked a smile.

The possibility that he will be elected at all is, of course, little better than the chance that Babe Ruth will come back as a designated hitter.

The statistics contained with the ballot read for Bouton: "10 years. 21–7 in 1963. Led AL in games started (37) in 1964. 2–0 in 1964 World Series." Overall, with the Yankees, the Seattle Pilots, the Houston Astros, and the Atlanta Braves, he won 62 games and lost 63.

Walter Johnson he wasn't. So why is Bouton on the ballot?

It happens that anyone who has played in 10 major league seasons from 1964 to 1978, and who has been retired for at least five years, is eligible for Hall of Fame consideration now.

Bouton qualifies because he made his unusual return to the big leagues in 1978 with Atlanta, having played his ninth season with Houston in 1970.

A writer may vote for as many as 10 men, and a player is elected if he appears on 75 percent of the ballots.

Whom would Bouton vote for?

He went down the list.

"Elston Howard," he said, "because of his consistently out-standing performance for a long time in a variety of positions.

"And Nelson Fox, for a great, long career, and Harmon Killebrew—the fat kid—and Jim Bunning and Don Drysdale, among the pitchers. Oh, Hoyt Wilhelm, my patron saint, the patron saint of all knuckleball pitchers. Wilhelm, absolutely."

He added Luis Aparicio and Maury Wills.

"And Roger Maris. The 61 home runs are worth consideration. Breaking Ruth's record. That singular contribution might be enough."

Anyone else? "Well, maybe Jim Bouton. Also for a singular contribution." He wasn't altogether joking, and perhaps he shouldn't be.

Among the criteria on the Hall of Fame ballot is item No. 4:

"Candidates shall be chosen on the basis of playing ability, integrity, sportsmanship, character, their contribution to the team on which they played, and to baseball in general."

"I think *Ball Four* made a contribution to baseball," Bouton said. "Whether baseball thinks so or not is another matter.

"Baseball owners think that a contribution to the game is to the bottom line. The book wasn't that, in the sense that a home run is. But I got thousands of letters from people telling me the positive effect the book had on their lives. It was published 13 years ago, and I still get two or three letters every day, especially from teenagers, who tell me that they identify with me as an underdog.

"They said they enjoyed how I struggled and yet could laugh about being a relief pitcher who was hanging on. It made them feel better about themselves. A lot of teenagers don't feel comfortable in the world. And *Ball Four* apparently gave them a feeling that they weren't alone.

"As a kid, I was always thought to be too small and skinny to make the big leagues. I imagined big-leaguers were from another planet."

Bouton would grow to 5'11½" and 170 pounds.

"When I made it to the Yankees," said Bouton, "it was like walking in this wonderland, this crazy place, but it was fun. I always felt that I was in the locker room by mistake, but felt privileged to be there. When I'd go back home after every season, I'd tell people about it—like it was this great adventure I'd been on—and I'd even regularly talk to church groups about it.

"With *Ball Four*, I never meant to make an investigation of a subculture. I just wanted to share the nonsense.

"But the book did go into things about ballplayers like Mickey Mantle playing in a game with a hangover, and players running on rooftops and looking into windows at girls. And about them taking greenies—the pills were like an industrial aid, to help performance. One time, for example, John Kennedy, a real mild-mannered infielder, kicked the water cooler in the dugout and tore the cover off it. Gary Bell, the pitcher, watched this and said, 'His pep pills just kicked in.'"

Bouton believes that, for the baseball establishment, "the crime of the book" was his account of how poorly ballplayers in general were being paid under the reserve system; the minimum salary then was under $10,000 a year. "It was hard to make a living in baseball then," he said.

"And I think it did take a new look, an honest look, at some of our heroes. And I guess it questions if heroes are such terrific things. Someone once said, 'Don't pity the nation that has no heroes, pity the nation that needs them.' People who don't feel good enough about themselves need to feel good about someone else.

"If you don't have an accurate view, then you don't see things clearly, and you miscalculate and build false expectations. Things don't happen by magic. And I thought it's better to know the truth."

Bouton now owns and markets his creation, Big League Cards, a gift or business item that allows anyone's picture and "personal statistics," like those of ballplayers, to be put on a card and packed with "real bubble gum."

"With these cards, everyone's his own hero," said Bouton. "Part of the fun of the business is seeing people celebrate themselves."

CONE MUST
PROVE HIMSELF AGAIN

April 13, 1998

SOMETIME BEFORE the thrill of the Yankees' coming back twice in the game yesterday afternoon to beat the Oakland A's plus Mariah Carey in the crowd exercising her expensive vocal chords while cheering for the object of her affections, the Yankee shortstop, a scenario played out in the Yankee bullpen that drew at least equal interest from management.

In the late-morning sunshine, David Cone threw in that familiar tight corkscrew motion. He threw for the first time since Friday, when he made the second of his two stunningly miserable starts to open the season. It is generally believed that Cone, whose heart and right arm are widely and deservedly adored by New York fans, must be one of the essential ingredients if there is to be bunting hanging in Yankee Stadium at World Series time.

And while the schedule tells us that there is still the small matter of some 152 games left in the regular season, some fans, and perhaps even one among the loftiest reaches of the Yankee hierarchy, may wonder: is it too soon to panic?

"I can't remember ever being this bad in the first two games of the season," Cone said. "Not even in Little League. I had a total of 12 runs to work with in the last game, and I never got past the fifth inning."

Cone was now seated before his locker in the Yankee clubhouse, sweat still pebbling his face. He has had two shoulder surgeries in the last two years—one for an aneurysm in 1996 and one for bursitis last October—and the concern for the health of his shoulder is palpable.

"I threw well, I feel great," Cone said, regarding his bullpen outing. "I've felt great all spring, and that's what makes what happened to me so strange. So you can't help having some anxiety about this."

He said he was reluctant to make excuses about his two starts— a loss to Oakland in which he blew a 3–0 lead and that last dreadful no-decision against Oakland in the Yankee home opener Friday. But he did complain that the cold, windy weather affected his ability to grip the ball on his put-away pitch, the slider. When he has two strikes on the batter, the slider is the pitch that generally sends the batter dragging back to the dugout. Instead, in his first two starts, the batters were racing gleefully about the bases.

The thing about starting pitchers in particular is that there is such a length between starts that the mind may play havoc with confidence, always a fragile commodity. Usually a starter gets to work every five days, but in the case of the 35-year-old Cone, that may be extended, said the Yankee manager, Joe Torre, to six days to give him more time to restore his aging muscles.

His next start is Wednesday against Anaheim.

"You always have to constantly prove yourself," Cone said. "You are only as good as your last start."

In Cone's case, there is more. The surgery for the aneurysm, he believes, has affected the circulation in his arm, accounting perhaps for the lack of feeling in his fingers while gripping the ball. "The ball felt glassy," he said.

The Yankee doctor, Stuart Hershon, believes that when the weather warms, so will Cone's bloodstream. The even greater problem for Cone's poor starts, he believes, is the consequence of the operation for bursitis. "We were projecting David to come back in May," Hershon said, "but he was so intense about his rehab— he's an incredible competitor—that he accelerated the time frame.

He was just so eager to come back. Now his muscle memory has to kick in—and that affects his mechanics."

In baseball argot, mechanics are to a pitcher what brush strokes are to a painter, with body and leg thrust added to arm extension and wrist flick.

"I give the batter a lot of looks—arm angles and pitches," Cone said, "and so in the bullpen I went back to basics, and tried to simplify." He stayed primarily with his overhand four-seam fastball and a single breaking pitch—"the good hard slider, which has been my forte over the years."

His forte has also been strikeouts—with a hugely comfortable strikeout-to-walk ratio, a most telling pitching statistic. In the nine and two-thirds innings he has pitched this season, he has given up six walks while striking out seven. He shook his head. "Ugly," he commented.

One remembers Cone, in his remarkable return from the career-threatening aneurysm, pitching no-hit ball for seven innings in his first start back in 1996; he is remembered for showing grit in playoff and World Series games; he is remembered for being a man of stature on the field and in the clubhouse.

And one views the virtually indomitable Cone and roots for his sake that the ball on a cold, windy day come October will not feel glassy to him.

CATFISH HUNTER: THE OBITUARY

September 10, 1999

CATFISH HUNTER, the Hall of Fame right-hander who helped pitch the Oakland A's and the Yankees to six pennants in the 1970s, hurled a perfect game, and was part of an economic revolution in sports, died yesterday at his home at Hertford, North Carolina. He was 53.

He had been struggling for the last year with amyotrophic lateral sclerosis, the progressive and ultimately fatal neurological condition also known as Lou Gehrig's disease. He had also been hospitalized after falling and hitting his head on concrete steps outside his home August 8. He was sent home Saturday.

Hunter was a premier pitcher of his era, a 6′, 190-pounder who did not have overpowering speed but possessed outstanding control, an assortment of superb pitches, and a winner's poise.

He won 224 games in 15 major league seasons from 1965 to 1979 and won at least 21 games over five consecutive seasons, from 1971 to 1974 with Oakland and in 1975 with the Yankees. He won the Cy Young Award as the American League's top pitcher in 1974 and was an eight-time All-Star. In compiling a record of 224–166, he had an outstanding career earned-run average of 3.26.

Although an unassuming ballplayer who rarely took himself seriously, Hunter was wise enough to become the first big-money free agent. An arbitrator freed him from his contract with Charlie Finley's Athletics after the 1974 season, and the Yankees signed him to a five-year, $3.35 million contract that was the largest in baseball history at that time.

While his case did not directly lead to free agency for other players—a ruling in an unrelated case the next year led to that—it showed the players what they, too, might command from the baseball owners.

"He paved the way for me," said Roger Clemens, who will earn $16.1 million with the Yankees over 1999 and 2000.

James Augustus Hunter was born on April 8, 1946, on a farm near Hertford in Perquimans County. He said he was taught to pitch by his older brothers.

"My three brothers taught me to throw strikes," he said when inducted into the Baseball Hall of Fame in 1987, "and thanks to them I gave up 379 home runs in the big leagues."

Hunter was overstating things a bit, having given up 374 homers. And the control he developed by throwing baseballs at a hole in the barn door—the last brother to hit the hole had to do the chores—would pay off.

A Yankee teammate, pitcher Pat Dobson, once said about Hunter, "He can put the ball where he wants it—or within an inch or two, which is just about as good. From that one capacity stems everything else."

On occasion, Hunter's family would travel to Baltimore to watch major league baseball. "I remember once we were watching Robin Roberts there," Hunter said, "and my father said, 'Hell, I could hit him; he's not throwing that hard.' We were sitting behind the plate, and Roberts really did look as though you could murder him. But nobody seemed to do it. I admired the heck out of Roberts. I just naturally patterned myself after him, and eventually I learned to do it, too."

Major league hitters would feel the same way about Hunter as Hunter's father had felt about Roberts. "I could never understand why I couldn't hit Hunter," said Ed Herrmann, an opponent who later became a teammate on the Yankees. "Even when you're up at the plate, you think, just give me one more of those and I'll clout it out of here. But I rarely did."

Hunter was known all his life as Jimmy in his home area. Finley, the A's flamboyant owner, gave him the nickname Catfish and apparently manufactured a story to go with it. "Around here, we never call him Catfish," Ray Ward, editor of the *Perquimans Weekly*, once said. "We call him Jimmy. Jimmy's mother has been upset about the nickname." The story created to go with the name: Hunter had once run away from home and come back with two catfish. "His mother was irritated that somebody would believe her little boy ran off," Ward said.

During Hunter's senior year at Perquimans High School in Hertford, he was wounded in his right foot when his brother Pete's shotgun misfired, destroying the little toe and leaving the foot full of pellets. The Kansas City Athletics signed him anyway, for a $50,000 bonus, and sent him to the Mayo Clinic for surgery. He spent the 1964 season on the disabled list, but the foot did not bother him after the operation even though about 15 shotgun pellets remained.

Hunter never pitched in the minor leagues, starting the 1965 season with a cellar-bound Kansas City team that had eight rookies. He had an 8–8 record that year and was 55–64 in his first five seasons, never finishing above .500. Despite his mediocre won-lost records with mostly mediocre A's teams, Hunter was named an American League All-Star in 1966 and 1967.

In 1968 Finley moved the A's to Oakland, and on May 8 of that year Hunter retired all 27 Minnesota Twins he faced, the first regular-season perfect game in the American League since 1922.

The fortunes of the A's improved dramatically after their move to Oakland, and they quickly developed into a powerhouse that won three straight World Series from 1972 to 1974. Hunter also improved, in part because of a slight modification to his pitching motion, and he became the steady center of a swaggering, squabbling club that featured larger-than-life characters like Reggie Jackson, Vida Blue, and Rollie Fingers. In his last five seasons with Oakland he compiled a record of 106–49, and he was 4–0 in seven World Series appearances.

Jackson, a teammate of Hunter's with both the A's and the Yankees, would recall, "When we started winning in Oakland, Cat was the father of those teams." Hunter was only 26 when the A's won their first World Series championship.

Lou Piniella was another teammate on the Yankees. "The main thing about Cat is that statistics didn't mean much to him," Piniella said. "The only thing that mattered was victories. He didn't have overpowering stuff, but he knew how to pitch and how to beat you. If there was a game you had to win, he's the guy you wanted on the mound."

After he won the Cy Young Award in 1974 with a record of 25–12 and a league-leading 2.49 ERA, Hunter uncovered a violation of his contract with Finley and the A's that allowed him to become a free agent. The A's were to send half of Hunter's $100,000 annual salary to a North Carolina bank as payment on an annuity, but Finley did not comply.

At season's end, with the guidance of the Players' Association, Hunter took a grievance to arbitration. He won and was declared a free agent, unfamiliar words in baseball in 1974. When he learned of the decision by telephone, Hunter hung up and, shaken, turned to his wife, Helen. "We don't belong to anybody," he told her.

"I was scared," Hunter recalled. "I didn't have a job. I didn't realize the implications."

His case was an anomaly; it was the next year before Andy Messersmith and Dave McNally would challenge baseball's reserve clause and win, establishing the players' union's power and spurring a tremendous escalation in athletes' salaries. But Hunter was about to show baseball players what their services were worth on the open market.

Hunter was the most accomplished veteran player ever to become a free agent, and soon teams were clamoring for his services in an unprecedented bidding war.

Among those who sought to sign him was Gene Autry, the singing cowboy of the movies who was the owner of the California Angels. Autry was so eager that he traveled across the country to meet Hunter in Ahoskie, North Carolina, 60 miles from Hertford.

"Gene Autry came down here handing out records of 'Rudolph the Red-Nosed Reindeer,'" Hunter once recalled. "That was the biggest thing that ever came to Ahoskie."

Twenty-three of the 24 teams in the major leagues—all but the San Francisco Giants—bid for Hunter's services. George Steinbrenner's $3.35 million offer to pitch for the Yankees for five years, which included a $1 million signing bonus and various insurance policies and annuities, was the most appealing, and the Yankees announced the signing of Hunter on New Year's Eve 1974.

The $150,000 annual salary Hunter received from the Yankees did not even rank among the top 10 in baseball—Dick Allen of the Chicago White Sox had received $250,000 in 1974. But the total package was the largest in baseball's history, and it made Hunter, at age 28, one of the three or four highest-paid American athletes at a time when rival leagues in hockey and football had already begun to drive up salaries.

But it was not just the money that brought Hunter to New York. "We'd had better offers, but New York was closer to home and they played on regular grass," he said. Coming to the Yankees also meant rejoining Clyde Kluttz, the scout who had signed Hunter to his first contract with Kansas City.

Hunter again led the league in victories in his first season with the Yankees, winning 23 games. He was 17–15 the following season, when the team won its first pennant in 12 years, and he compiled records of 9–9 and 12–6 for the Yankees' World Series winning teams of 1977 and 1978, despite spending time on the disabled list during both seasons.

He was a humorous and a stabilizing force in the clubhouse for the Yankees, as he had been for the A's. While his jokes to teammates could be pointed, they were usually taken well. When Jackson had a candy bar named for him, Hunter said, "When you unwrap one, it tells you how good it is."

When Hunter was elected to the Hall of Fame, Steinbrenner, the Yankees' principal owner, said, "You started our success. You were the first to teach us how to win. Other Yankees continued that leadership role, but you were the one who first showed us what it means to be a winner."

Hunter retired from baseball at age 33 when his contract expired after the 1979 season, having suffered problems with his pitching arm. But he found it no hardship to leave the limelight and return to his roots. Shortly after he joined the Yankees, he had said, "I don't like New York much, either. I had to live in a hotel downtown for a couple of months until my wife got here. Hated it. Now I got this nice home in Norwood, New Jersey, and I just drive straight from there to the ballpark. Never go downtown. Nothing for me to do down there."

Hunter and his wife, Helen, his high school sweetheart, lived in the same house outside tiny Hertford for more than 20 years. But their 100 acres had increased to 1,000. He was a full-time farmer in his corn, soybean, and peanut fields for 10 years after he retired from baseball, and then he turned it over to a friend who leased the land.

He was an avid fisherman and hunter, keeping a kennel of deer hounds and bird dogs and shooting quail, pheasant, rabbit, and deer in the winter.

The financial package from the Yankees in 1974 included $25,000 payments for annuities for college tuition for his two children, Todd, then five, and Kimberly, two. His son Paul was born five years later. "I forgot I might have one more after baseball," Hunter said. "I have to pay for him myself."

In addition to his wife and three children, Hunter is survived by three brothers, three sisters, and a grandson.

Hunter was a fierce competitor, but he kept his perspective and his unruffled disposition, understanding that baseball was just a game. "Golf's the only thing that makes me mad," he once said, with a smile.

Hunter entered a hospital in Baltimore last September after experiencing difficulties with motor skills, and amyotrophic lateral sclerosis was diagnosed. He did not appear in public outside his hometown again until March, when he attended the Yankees' first spring training game in Tampa, Florida. He joked with reporters but had difficulty shaking hands.

"I've got no strength in my arms and my hands," he said last fall. "I can't do the routine things like button a shirt anymore."

Helen Hunter helped him with cutting his food and tying his shoes. "I'm putting a lot of work on her, and she's strong," Catfish Hunter said. "But once in a while we sit here and cry together."

For many of his friends and family and teammates, Hunter's charm was memorable. After he lost a game with the Yankees in the 1977 World Series, for example, he was unhappy but not distraught. He understood that there are good days and bad.

"The sun," he said, "don't shine on the same dog all the time."

IV.

THE HOT SEAT

TORRE KNOWS VICTORY ISN'T EVERYTHING

October 28, 2003

IT WAS SOMETIME earlier in the season, and I was walking down the runway extending from the Yankees' locker room to the dugout at Yankee Stadium. A large printed sign had been hung overhead about midway through. It read, "There Is No Substitute for Victory."

You notice these so-called inspiration signs in locker rooms and perhaps even boardrooms, but rarely do you pay attention to them. I had probably seen the sign numerous times but simply paid no attention to it, as I imagine the Yankees hadn't. Except, that is, for one Yankee in particular.

"Oh, that was put up at the direction of George," said Joe Torre, the Yankees' manager, when the sign was mentioned to him. George, to be sure, is George Steinbrenner, the principal owner, who hovers over the team like a bloated black cloud. "He likes those kinds of things."

Torre gave no indication of the effectiveness of such a motto of encouragement, just objectively stated the origin of its presence.

But I wondered about the essence of "There Is No Substitute for Victory." I said to Torre, "What about inner peace?"

I was only half-joking, thinking that no one could really take the sign totally seriously, it being so lacking in perspective, unless, surely, you were in a combat, or fighting for your survival in some similar fashion. But baseball, that game of ball and stick with the participants wearing knickers? (In fact, the quotation comes from Gen. Douglas MacArthur, who said, "In war, there is no substitute for victory." Steinbrenner just left out the first part.)

"Inner peace?" Torre said. "Absolutely."

Torre's face went from almost bemusement at the sign to one of dead seriousness.

He began talking of his childhood, in Brooklyn, with a father who was abusive to him, to his siblings, and especially to his mother. "I remember coming home in the evening and seeing his car parked in front of our house, and not wanting to go in," Torre said. "Sometimes I didn't."

He said that experience motivated him to start, with his wife, Ali, the Joe Torre Safe at Home Foundation, which will raise money to educate the public about abuse in families.

So parental love may be, for Joe Torre, more important than victory. Human consideration may be, for Joe Torre, more important than victory. Helping those who need help may also be, for Joe Torre, more important than victory.

Which isn't to say that victory isn't important to Joe Torre. Ask any of his players and they'll tell you that few hate losing as much as Joe Torre, and few want to win as much as Joe Torre. It's just that, unlike Steinbrenner, apparently, Torre doesn't issue dire statements that, for example, there will be hellfire to pay just because a team goes to Game 6 of the World Series and loses to the Marlins. Steinbrenner wasn't as preposterous after this year's Series loss as he was in 1981 when he "apologized" to the people of New York after the Dodgers beat the Yankees.

He has now promised changes, and some are surely needed. But every team seeks to make changes. The Marlins will make changes. For everything, so we've been told, there is a season. Life marches on, and so forth.

Torre has been hugely successful as manager of the Yankees. The fact that his team has now lost two World Series in the last three seasons hardly negates the fact that he's won four World Series and six pennants in his eight years as Yankees manager.

A lot of teams haven't been in any World Series in that time. One, for example, hasn't played in the season finale in 57 years—oops, 58, counting this year.

Why has Torre been so extraordinarily successful managing the Yankees?

Because, say people close to the team, he gets the best out of the players. He does that by not being confrontational—unlike, oh, a certain owner. He never embarrasses a player in public. And, in most instances, he remains calm—intense, yes; thoughtful, yes; but also calm. The players pick up on this. They trust him, and trust his actions and reactions. They are more relaxed, while remaining competitive. Tight players fail.

When Torre was away from his home as a youth, he was more relaxed. He was a talented athlete and understood the importance of staying away from unnecessarily imposed pressure. There are numerous reasons why a ballplayer makes it to the major leagues, and Joe Torre obviously fulfilled some of them and had a terrific playing career.

He had modest success as a manager with the Mets, the Braves, and the Cardinals before taking over the Yankees. But his managerial reign has been the longest consecutive tenure by far in the mercurial, impulsive Steinbrenner era.

It seems apparent that Torre understands what bullying is, coming from the kind of home that he did, and so, as an adult, he knows how to deal with it. Don Zimmer, Torre's bench coach, quit Sunday because he said he had become fed up with Steinbrenner, that Steinbrenner didn't treat him "as a human being."

Torre said the other day that he planned to stay on because "it's still electric for me to get into the dugout, and you are still excited."

"As long as that happens, I don't think I can walk away from it," he added. "The players make it worthwhile."

There wasn't anything about victory at any cost. It was about the game, and about the people. It was Joe Torre, who as a boy learned about perspective the hard way, seeing things for what they are.

TIME AND SUCCESS
MELLOW PINIELLA

August 17, 2002

CHICAGO — When Lou Piniella—"Sweet Lou" to Yankee fans—was named manager of the Yankees in 1986, at age 42 just a year and a half removed from his playing career and with no managerial experience, he thought he was in a great situation, especially since he was on good terms with the owner, George Steinbrenner.

"Was I in for a surprise," recalled Piniella, now the Seattle Mariners' manager. "There was that red phone on my desk. And it would ring and it would be George, with lineup suggestions. And with comments on the previous game. It was infuriating.

"One time, he said to me, 'Whenever you want to take a pitcher out, leave him in. And whenever you want to leave a pitcher in, take him out.'

"Oh boy. I said to him, 'Mr. Steinbrenner, I know you were once an assistant football coach at Northwestern University.' He said, 'That's right.' I said, 'And you were pretty good?' He said, 'Yes.' I said, 'You prepared them for that tie game so well that they forgot about the other nine games.' Northwestern went 0–9–1 that year. I'd get his goat." Piniella laughed and then shrugged. "And, of course, eventually he fired me."

Piniella wasn't the only manager Steinbrenner ever fired. Still, Piniella, who won 90 and 89 games with the Yankees in two full seasons before being dismissed midway through a third, finds room for self-criticism now. "I fought George. Looking back," he said, with some understatement, "I realize it was not the right approach."

Times change. Piniella is about to turn 59, is gray about the temples and has learned a lot more about managing and handling situations since those early days with the Yankees. He is in his 16th season as a big-league manager, and he has had considerable success, winning a World Series with the Cincinnati Reds in 1990. He took over a moribund Mariners team 10 seasons ago—"I was told by friends, 'Don't take the job, you'll die there'"—and has had them contending for much of the time. The Mariners have played in the American League Division Series four times and the ALCS three times, losing the last two years to the Yankees.

"They've derailed us, and that's been a frustration," Piniella said. "You put on this uniform to win, to win it all. And every year you think—hope—this is the year."...

Piniella has developed such a superb reputation that Ken Harrelson, the former player who is now a Chicago White Sox broadcaster, said, "Lou is the best manager in baseball. He could go into any dugout and get the job done."

Piniella has succeeded in Seattle despite the loss of some of the best players in baseball—Randy Johnson, Ken Griffey Jr., and Alex Rodriguez. "You don't want to get attached to players, but sometimes you can't help it," Piniella said, then added with a smile, "especially if they're very good."

He has kept the team winning this season, despite injuries to several important players, including designated hitter Edgar Martinez, who was out for two months. Yet the Mariners are again on top of the AL West, though in a battle with Anaheim and Oakland.

Piniella has constructed a compelling team, popular enough in Seattle to be on its way to drawing 3 million fans for the third straight season, behind only the Yankees in attendance this season.

Piniella recently reflected on the Yankees and their manager, Joe Torre.

"I marvel at Joe," Piniella said in the manager's office in Comiskey Park recently before a Mariners–White Sox game. "He's the model of consistency. He appears so serene in the dugout, but I know he has to be churning inside. He also has a bit of the river-boat gambler in him. He's a little unorthodox at times—he'll steal when you wouldn't expect him to, he'll hit and run when you wouldn't think he would. You can't catnap in the dugout when you manage against Joe Torre. It's a challenge.

"And he knows how to deal with the owner—he gets whatever he wants, within reason, that is."

Piniella and Steinbrenner have retained a friendship.

"I owe my managerial career to George," Piniella said. "He made me the manager, and it was on-the-job training. He saw something in me—I know he liked my intensity as a player—and he gave me a shot."

When the Yankees beat the Mariners in the ALCS in 2000, Piniella said, "George was the first one to come to the clubhouse and congratulate me. He said, 'You've done a great job in Seattle.' I appreciated that."

But Piniella couldn't quite let well enough alone. "George is a great winner. And when he congratulated me, I said, 'Thanks, George, you sent us home again.' I don't know if he would have been there if we had won."

How has Piniella developed as a manager? "Winning is an atti-tude," he said. "And you have to instill it if it's not quite there. Two things are needed: the players have to have confidence in your abil-ity to manage, and you have to have a happy clubhouse."

The ins and outs of managing, he said, were taught to him by Billy Martin—"my mentor." As for the happy clubhouse—something Martin rarely had—Piniella said, "I had to learn that on my own."

Piniella emphasizes versatility among his players. Like bunting. "We practice bunting every day," he said. "And in the last two months, we won two games with squeeze bunts."

Mike Cameron, the center fielder, said, "When you see him doing things like that, it gives you confidence that he knows what he's doing. In a playoff game my first year with Seattle, Lou came out of the dugout to talk to me when I got on first base. I had no idea what he was doing. He said, 'If the catcher steps outside, don't steal. If he doesn't, go.' He didn't, and I stole second."

When third baseman Jeff Cirillo was thrown out trying to stretch a single, Piniella got on him. Cirillo said, "I told him, 'I went to draw the throw so that the runner ahead of me could score. And besides, the first-base coach waved me on.' Lou said, 'I apologize.' You appreciate that in a manager. He had the confidence in himself to admit a wrong. And if I'm wrong, 'Hey, it's my bad.'"

Piniella said he wanted the players relaxed in the clubhouse, and he often relies on his veterans to set a tone.

Piniella said that in his earlier years, he misdirected some of his intensity. "I was a little too confrontational at times," he said. "Like I had a problem with John Candelaria, when I was with the Yankees. We didn't speak for the last six weeks of the season. Now, I'd call him in my office, and we'd hash it out properly."

During his championship season with the Reds, Piniella got into a scuffle in the locker room with reliever Rob Dibble. "I liked Rob, and he was a real competitor," Piniella said. "We had discussed a particular thing, and I thought it was straightened out. Then it happened again, and I blew a gasket. That's something I'd never do again. Basically, I had to learn it."

Piniella says he still makes mistakes, however. "When we lose a game, I drive home thinking of all the options I could have taken and didn't, to win," he said. "Many a night, I drive by my exit."

As for Piniella's famed temper and tantrums—few kicked dirt around umpires with his artistry—he said, "I've mellowed a bit. I'm almost 60 years old, and my wife, Anita, has given me stern lectures. She said, 'Do you have to make a fool of yourself—again?'" Piniella threw back his head and laughed that great laugh, the opposite of those temper tantrums.

"I've only had one really big blowout this season, and it was in Tampa, where I grew up," he said. "My parents were in the front row. And I guess I wanted to remind them what I was like in the sandbox."

And the manager's office was again filled with laughter.

RUBBERNECKING ON BILLY DAY

August 11, 1986

"WHAT ARE YOU doing today?" a friend asked. "Going to Yankee Stadium." "Who's playing?"

"The Royals, and it's Billy Martin Day. They're putting a plaque of Martin in the outfield." "You're kidding." "No, it's true."

"They're putting a plaque of Billy Martin out there with the plaques of Ruth and Gehrig and DiMaggio and Mantle and those guys?" "Yeah." There was a pause on the phone. "It's…it's sacrilegious," the friend said. He wasn't aware that there were also two plaques commemorating the visit to Yankees Stadium of two Popes. "I mean," he continued, "why are they honoring this man?" "I'm not sure," came the reply. The question the friend had posed was a good one, one that was being asked by numerous people when they learned of these quizzical pregame goings-on. And so in the pursuit of journalistic thoroughness, a journey was made to Yankee Stadium, this mecca and symbol of all that is virtuous and pure in American life.

At the beginning of the ceremonies, the attention of the 45,000 or so fans was directed to the Diamond Vision screen in center field. There the fans were treated to a filmed collection of selected scenes from Billy Martin's baseball career, as player and manager.

Here he made his diving catch in the 1953 World Series to save the day, and there he was at bat (he was a career .257 hitter), and there he's arguing with an umpire, and here he's arguing with an umpire, and there he's kicking dirt on an umpire, and here he's got his baseball cap turned sideways and he's screaming in an umpire's face, and there he's chasing an umpire and waving his arms madly, and now he's kicking more dirt on an umpire, and more, and more. A lot of people, who got lost on their way to *Rambo*, cheered.

Billy Martin had kicked up so much dirt, in fact, that he dug his own grave numerous times in baseball. The film didn't say that Martin was let go by the Yankees four times. It didn't say that he was booted out as manager of the Twins and Tigers and Rangers and A's, too.

It didn't say that he was always being picked on in bars—his version—and forced to fight with, here, a reporter and, there, a marshmallow salesman. Oh, and in this corner a pitcher. Last year, when both were drinking one late night in a hotel bar—Martin was then the Yankee manager in Tour No. 4—he fought Ed Whitson. In one of the marvelous quotes of the season, Martin shouted at Whitson, who was coming at him with a look of wild hatred in his eyes, "What's wrong with you, can't you hold your liquor?"

In the film clip, not a word about calling George Steinbrenner a convicted liar, and Reggie Jackson a born liar, and then saying he didn't say it when it was reported, and implying that the reporters were liars. And then later admitting he had said it, which put into question who the on-the-record liar was.

He has his fans, to be sure. In 15 years as a manager, he won five division titles, with four teams, and took the Yankees to two World Series, winning one and losing one. He was aggressive, if not always tactful. Some players liked him very much, some would rather have taken cod-liver oil for a cocktail than play for him.

Now, Martin's family came out and gathered around home plate, and met Billy, who stood with a quiet smile and tan suit and striped tie and a carnation in his lapel. His mother greeted him, and his brothers and sisters and son and daughter, and two grandchildren, followed by a lot of people showering Martin with gifts, including a set of four tires to a convertible automobile to something else presented him by a lady wearing a hat dripping with bananas, and who was representing, surprisingly enough, a banana company.

There was stuff about his "distinguished" career and how he did it "with dignity" and was a "credit on the field as well as off."

Now, more film clips of him kicking dirt on umpires. And then a real live former umpire, Ron Luciano, came out and brought a gift and prominently mentioned the sponsor and then tossed down a box of dirt—from each infield in the American League, he said— and gave Billy "a free kick at a lousy umpire." Martin rolled up his pants leg and kicked meekly. Everyone on the field got a big guffaw out of this.

It was kind of strange, but fascinating. Overdone? Yes. But much of Billy has been overdone. Compelling? Well, in the way that watching a traffic accident is compelling. You rubberneck despite yourself.

In a news conference afterward, someone wondered why he had been given this honor.

He mentioned that, well, maybe it was his managing, mostly, and a little of his baseball playing.

But there had to be more, someone suggested. "I guess," said Martin, "that some of the fans relate to me as a piece of every one of them—the guy in the street being aggressive, fighting their boss. I fought what I thought was right, and couldn't worry about what City Hall thought."

George Steinbrenner, whose brainstorm this Day was, said that he felt Billy deserved it because "being a Yankee has never meant more to anyone than it has to Billy Martin." Is that a reason to enshrine him? "I felt he deserved it," said Steinbrenner. "I'm tired of flowers for the dead. I like flowers for the living."

Did you notice, he was asked, that many fans were stirred most by the scenes of him kicking dirt on umpires?

"You've got to have a sense of humor about this," he said. "I mean, there are really serious things out there—there's hunger and unemployment and wars...."

And so Billy Martin Day came to a close, and a Yankee ball-game, without Billy Martin managing the local team, began. Later, at home, the phone rang. It was the friend. "Well, did you find out why they honored that man?" he asked. "Because of flowers," came the reply. "Flowers?"

"Sure, flowers for the living. Got it straight from Steinbrenner."

REMEMBERING
BILLY MARTIN, BATTLER

December 30, 1989

ALL AROUND TOWN yesterday, on a cold late December morning, Christmas decorations, still cheery, remained in evidence. Near the corner of Madison and 51st Street, about a block from St. Patrick's Cathedral, the taxi slowed because of a police barricade and heavy traffic.

"Must be the funeral for the ballplayer," the driver said. "What's his name?" "Billy Martin," she was told. "I'm not a sports fan," she said, "but I heard about him, heard how he died. So stupid. Him and his pal driving after drinking. Thank God no innocent people got hurt."

Billy Martin, according to reports, had been drinking at a bar on Christmas Day with a friend near Martin's farm home in Upstate New York. At around 6:00 in the evening, the friend, William Reedy, driving Martin's pickup truck, with Martin in the passenger's seat, spun off an icy road and crashed. Martin, not wearing a seat belt, was thrown through the windshield and killed. He was 61 years old.

There seems now some kind of celebration, some great homage to Billy Martin, who, say his supporters, was a man of the people, the little guy who fought the big guy, a winner, "a true Yankee."

There were two days of viewings at a funeral parlor in Manhattan, and a line of fans stood in the cold to bid him farewell.

Some were deeply moved, including his pal and teammate in the 1950s, Whitey Ford.

"I didn't hear about it until 6:00 in the morning," said Ford. "A reporter called and asked what I thought about what happened to Billy Martin. I said, 'What did Billy do now?' When I heard, I said I couldn't talk, and hung up. I didn't answer the phone the rest of the day."

Willie Randolph, who played for Martin during Martin's five turns at managing the Yankees, said Martin was no angel.

"But I always thought he had a good heart," said Randolph.

Randolph and Ford were honorary pallbearers, and, along with Mickey Mantle and George Steinbrenner and five others, wheeled Martin's coffin into St. Patrick's for the Mass. Some 3,000 people packed the church, including Martin's widow, Jill, his daughter, Kelly, and his son, Billy Joe. Richard M. Nixon was there, and Bill Skowron, Ron Guidry, Don Mattingly, Phil Rizzuto, and Chris Chambliss, as well as those standing several deep along the side altars.

Besides his pugnacious ballplaying and combative managing, Martin was famous for unsavory incidents. Some considered him a great fighter when he kicked dirt on umpires. Some thought him feisty when he stood up to the principal owner. But he kept coming back for more, and it seemed demeaning.

As for being a "true Yankee," something Martin liked to call himself, no one would have mistaken his demeanor for that of the elegant DiMaggio, the patient Mattingly, the reserved Gehrig. Perhaps Martin, who won some and lost some, saw it more as a craving for winning.

Martin drank. He drank regularly, and regularly drank to excess. He engaged in bar brawls with people from a marshmallow salesman to his pitcher Ed Whitson, who broke the manager's arm. "Billy," said Denny McLain recently, "always got in the first punch."

Nor was Martin always a stand-up guy. He said he didn't hit the marshmallow man, and later admitted he had. He said he didn't call the boss a liar—he accused reporters of making it up—and later admitted he had.

With Billy, said Bishop Edwin Broderick, in his opening remarks yesterday, you got a lot of "thrills and spills, ups and downs," but "he was always, one must admit, an interesting show." Mickey Mantle, holding a white handkerchief, wiped his eyes, and his nose.

The Bishop spoke of Martin as a sentimentalist, a soft touch for old ballplayers down on their luck, and said that he always carried in his pocket a crumpled prayer card of St. Jude. "That was Billy's favorite saint," said the Bishop. "The saint of the impossible."

To many, Martin was impossible, too. The Bishop called him "an unforgettable character."

Martin's last public appearance was last week when, with the Tampa Symphony and Steinbrenner, he participated in a Christmas benefit for underprivileged children in Florida. Martin, in blue suit and reading glasses, recited "'Twas the Night Before Christmas."

"We worked real hard on that," Jill Martin had recalled. "It's a real tongue twister."

"I told Billy," recalled Steinbrenner, "'If you screw this up, it's the end of your lifetime contract.' He laughed, and said, 'Pressure, pressure, pressure.' He pointed to the Santa Claus suit I was wearing and said, 'That's nice, George. You didn't need a pillow.'"

Now at St. Patrick's, Bishop Broderick concluded the Mass. "May he rest in peace," he said.

Then the pallbearers stood, gathered and rolled Billy Martin's coffin out of the church.

"STAINED-GLASS" CASEY STENGEL

August 2, 1968

CASEY STENGEL said he recently celebrated his 78th birthday. The baseball record book says it oughta be 79. No matter. Casey is one of those rare birds who never grows old. That's because he's never been young.

For proof, note the following account by Damon Runyon of how Casey Stengel, then 33 (or 34), hit an inside-the-park home run in the ninth inning to win the first game of the 1923 World Series, 5–4, for the Giants over the Yankees:

> This is the way old Casey Stengel ran yesterday afternoon, running his home run home....
>
> *His mouth wide open.*
> *His warped old legs bending beneath him at every stride.*
> *His arms flying back and forth like those of a man swimming with a crawl stroke.*
> *His flanks heaving, his breath whistling, his head far back.*
>
> Yankee infielders passed by old Casey Stengel as he was running his home run home, adjuring himself to greater speeds as a jockey mutters to his horse in a race, swore that he was saying "Go on Casey! Go on!"

Runyon added Stengel's "warped old legs...just barely held out" until he reached the plate. "Then they collapsed," wrote Runyon.

Three thousand miles away in California, Edna Lawson, Stengel's fiancée, proudly showed newspaper clippings of Casey's game-winning blow to her father. "What do you think of my Casey?" she asked.

Her father shook his head. "I hope," he said, "that your Casey lives until the wedding." Edna and Casey were married the following August, and Casey's warped old legs even made it up the aisle. ("For the bridegroom," Casey said at the time, "it is the best catch he ever made in his career.")

Casey Stengel sat in the New York Met dugout at Shea Stadium prior to the recent Old-Timers' Game there. If accounts by Runyon and others of his day even border on accuracy, then Casey has not changed appreciably. If he could run a home run home then, he could probably do it now, too.

His white hair is sun-tinged in spots. A wave flaps over the side of his face, which is wrinkled like a rutted road. His blue eyes water now and then and he wipes them with a handkerchief as big as a flag. His tasteful blue suit is specked with light brown and looks almost natty on him.

And his legs. Of course, his warped old legs. He crosses them at the knee, and one works nervously under black executive socks. On his feet are black slippers. A young man wonders if old Casey Stengel wasn't shod in them when he ran his home run nearly half a century ago.

Old friends greeted Casey. Younger fellows introduced themselves to a legend in the parchment flesh. Some players that played for Casey when he managed the Amazin' Mets dropped by to chat briefly. And Casey talked. Someone has described Everett Dirksen as having a "stained-glass voice." If that is so, then Casey's voice is cracked stained-glass. And his syntax is as cloudy as rubbings from time-worn churchyard tombstones.

About the lack of hitting in the majors this year, Casey said, "They ask you, you ask yourself, I ask you, it's them good young pitchers between 18 and 24 years of age that can throw the ball over the plate and don't kill the manager, isn't it?"

About the St. Louis Cardinals: "St. Louis can execute and do more for ya. I thought Baltimore was going to be something but I quit on 'em, and then I thought Pittsburgh would excel but I quit on them, too.

"But you gotta admit they can run, St. Louis, I mean. Yeah, we'll say they can run. And they got two left-handers who'll shock ya and now the right-hander is commencing to be like Derringer or some of the others was. And a three-gamer, too. Can pitch every third day. The center fielder is a helluva good player and the left fielder is doin' an amazin' job. The fella at third they always worry about but he's doin' everything anyone could want. The first baseman got lotsa power and the catcher's now throwin' out people."

An old sportswriter friend came by and said he had just seen Edna in the stands and she's looking great as always.

Old Casey Stengel, who ran a home run home nearly half a century ago, jumped up on those warped old legs in black slippers and grabbed the old friend's hand.

Stengel's gnarled face beamed. "You got it, kid," he said, pumping the man's hand. "You sure do."

CLYDE KING FACES
ANOTHER CHALLENGE

August 5, 1982

ONE AFTERNOON IN 1932 when Clyde King was a seven-year-old boy in Goldsboro, North Carolina, he happened by a chicken yard, heard some commotion, and decided to take a look. He raised himself up and peeked over the fence. When he did, a dog leaped up and bit him around the right eye, and then took a ferocious bite of his forehead.

The incident remains with King, in several ways. He bears a long scar on his forehead, his right eye is weak and he wears thick glasses to correct his sight, and he's a man who understands that where there's a lot of squawking, there might also be a lot of trouble.

So what was Clyde King, 57 years old, graying, not on a noticeable diet, doing filling the manager's leather chair in the Yankee dressing room, replacing Gene Michael? Michael was deposed early yesterday. King becomes the third manager of the team this season, and the 10th in 10 years, which hardly begins to describe the uproar and flying feathers in the great chicken yard in the Bronx.

"George asked me if I'd do him a favor," said King, referring to George Steinbrenner, the Yankees' bull-terrier of an owner. "He asked me if I'd take over the team, and I said I would."

King says he is an organization man and has filled numerous roles for the Yankees since he joined them in 1976. He had most recently been Steinbrenner's special assistant.

He is called "interim" manager, which means whatever Steinbrenner's lexicon determines it to mean. "On the way out to the ballpark this afternoon, my wife, Norma, asked me if I was nervous coming to the ballpark today," said King, in the manager's office in Yankee Stadium. "I said no. If this had been my first job in baseball, or something, I might have. But I've been in the game for 38 years, and in almost every phase."

He has managed two other big-league teams, and considers managing a challenge, although an imminently transient one. Once he took the Giants to a second-place finish, and the Braves to third place. He got his jobs because he was respected for his careful approach to things—thinking, now, before he acted.

Yesterday, he had closed-door meetings with several players, believing that communication is essential. "Has Nettles gotten here yet?" he asked someone. About Rudy May, the left-handed pitcher who had expressed anger with the front office recently, King had only the warmest praise.

As a pitching coach with the Yankees, King understood that sometimes the best way to handle a situation is to not thrust yourself into it.

Shane Rawley, the Yankee pitcher, was impressed that King never came to him with various suggestions for changes, but when he had problems about a month ago, he went to King.

"With most established pitchers—and I've been in the major leagues for five years—when you're going bad, it's usually some small thing that's the matter," said Rawley. "I asked Clyde if he'd take a look, and he thought I should make a slight alteration in my grip. I did, and it made a difference. You see it in my record."

As a right-handed pitcher with Brooklyn in the mid-1940s and early 1950s, King hung on in the major leagues for seven years despite only average ability.

"Young man," Branch Rickey, the Brooklyn owner, said to him, "your head is two years ahead of your arm." "And it never caught up," says King, smiling. Facing the young, prodigious

Willie Mays for the first time, King knew he was in trouble. So when Mays tapped the plate with his bat, King threw. Strike one. Mays protested, but there was no rule against it. King had used a quick throw from a stretch position. Leo Durocher, the Giant manager coaching at third base, shouted at Willie to be ready.

When Mays looked back, strike two sailed past. Leo shouted again, and as Mays stepped back into the box, strike three crossed the plate. King, whose best record in the big leagues was 14–7 in 1951, may not be in the record book, but his influence is in the rule book: shortly after he struck out Mays, the rule was established that the batter must be ready before the pitcher can throw.

But that trick was child's play compared to a couple other of his moves. Pitching for the University of North Carolina in 1944, King would turn his cap slightly to the left when a runner got on first. "He couldn't tell if I was looking at him or the plate," said King.

The best was yet to come. His masterpiece—he swears it's true—came in a basketball game when he was in college. He had noticed that the man who would be guarding him always looked at his opponent's feet.

King, 6′ tall, borrowed a left sneaker from his team's 6′10″ center, and put it on his right foot. "It looked to the guy guarding me that I was going left when I kept going right," said King. "I scored five baskets in the first quarter. But I only scored two the rest of the game. The guy caught on."

DALLAS GREEN ISN'T BLUE

August 5, 1989

THIS IS THE TIME of year the manager of the Yankees traditionally wears a look like a raccoon, with big dark circles around his eyes. These somber shadows are brought on by fatigue, anguish, grief, and dyspepsia, all of which are synonyms for George Steinbrenner.

This is the time of year the manager also traditionally develops hollow pockets in his cheeks, a sickly complexion on his face, and a funny little tic. He looks as if he has just hit his head against the wall, or is about to, for the sheer pleasure of it. All this is brought on by sturm and drang, synonyms for George Steinbrenner.

Yet this year's manager of the Yankees, Dallas Green, retains a shockingly sanguine physiognomy. Oh, sure, his eyes revolve in their sockets a little faster than normal, but still not like the swift spin cycle of his predecessors. And there's the expected gnashing of teeth. But the cheeks retain a rose, and the step its spring.

The question was put to him: How is it that you look, well, not like a cadaver? "Why should I?" he asked. Why shouldn't you? came the reply.

"I was born and raised in this kind of business," he said, "and I don't let this"—he used an expletive—"bother me." The expletive referred to the recent remarks by Storm and Stress Steinbrenner, in which the team's owner said that the players were performing with intensity but that the manager and the coaches had to "show me" something more "if we are going to have a chance to win." Legitimately, Green has countered that if the players are doing well, then perhaps the manager and coaches could take some credit for it.

"If he's using it as a motivating tool for the coaching staff," said Green, "he's wasting an awful lot of time. This is the hardest-working coaching staff you could assemble."

He said that, yes, he can understand the frustration because he and his coaches want to win as much as the principal owner. But it was the method, the carping through the media, that he had a problem with. "I guess you just have to consider the source," he said.

He spoke calmly. He added, "The statement that Manager George"—a sweet sardonic touch—"made about game situations is a very logical second-guess. And hindsight always being 20-20, that's why managers get gray."

And Green is gray. But he is not blue. The team, despite a talent pool of less than Herculean strength when he took over as manager in the spring (a group of players for which Storm and Stress Steinbrenner must take responsibility), is still in the running for the American League East title.

Green said he is also unhappy that "the boss" doesn't talk to him directly about these problems. "But that's okay, because Syd's my boss, too, and he communicates with him," he said.

Syd is Syd Thrift, the general manager of the Yankees since March 21. Yankee general managers traditionally get bounced as rapidly as field managers. Thrift recalls first coming to town and riding in a cab with his wife. They were discussing where to live. When they were getting out, the cab driver turned to them and said, "Don't buy, rent."

In fact, Thrift has taken up residence in a midtown hotel. He admits to getting a lot of phone calls from Storm and Stress Steinbrenner. What do they talk about? "Everything from toothpicks to horse collars," he said. You do what? "That's a sayin' we had when I was growin' up in Locust Hill, Virginia," said Thrift. "It's got a population of a hundred, and my father was the postmaster and owned the general merchandise store. He'd say we had everything in the store from toothpicks to horse collars."

The conversations with Steinbrenner—they are mostly, he admitted, about baseball—can be unsettling. "But at this time of year, in a pennant race," said Thrift, "you always feel tension."

One day recently he looked in the mirror and said to himself, "Do I look this bad? Have I always looked this bad? Or is it getting badder?"

He also looked around him in a stadium box recently and noted there were four general managers there—that is, three ex: Gene Michael, Lou Piniella, and Bob Quinn. And two more in the dugout, Green and Charlie Fox. In the box, he said, "Maybe there's too many chiefs and not enough Indians." It drew a laugh. Plus, he noted, there were 11 managers—10 ex—in the box, on the field, and among the scouts.

Then there's Storm and Stress himself, who can never get his hiring quite right, seeking attention, veiling threats, trying to elbow the Mets from the top of the sports pages.

When the phone rings in your office, Thrift was asked, who do you immediately think is calling?

"It ain't Alexander Graham Bell," he said.

V.

THE WAY IT WAS

TWENTY-FIVE YEARS FAIL TO DIM
EITHER TITLE OR TURMOIL

July 7, 2002

IT WAS, as Cliff Johnson, one of the members of the 1977 Yankee team, recalled yesterday, a dysfunctional functional team. It was as though the inmates had taken over the asylum, and the asylum became the paradigm. In baseball terms, despite fights, conflicts, jealousies, antagonisms, and, it appeared at times, malice toward all, the Yankees won the championship.

Twenty-five years later, some 15 of those players assembled at Yankee Stadium yesterday for a celebration of that World Series victory, with the special feature of a home-plate ceremony to dedicate a plaque for Monument Park in honor of Reggie Jackson, who was the centerpiece of much of that madness, and a great deal of the success.

The earliest memory for Johnson, a backup catcher on that team, came in his first game on the Yankee bench when he was traded to the team in June. It was the infamous nationally televised game in Boston in which Billy Martin, the irascible manager, thought Jackson had loafed for a fly ball in right field and replaced him in mid-inning.

"I was sitting there, and Reggie comes into the dugout and he confronts Billy," Johnson said, "and they are about to go at it when Elston Howard jumps up to hold Reggie back, and Yogi Berra jumps up to hold Billy back. After the game, I called my mother in San Antonio. I said, 'Mom, these guys are crazy.'"

Ron Guidry, the wonderful, whippy left-handed pitcher on the team, said he was sitting right in front of Howard and Jackson.

"I was kicking Elston," Guidry said, "and whispering, 'Let them go at it!' Ah, yes. That team sure was a lot of fun. And on the bus trips, anything went."

Like Mickey Rivers, the center fielder. He spoke so swiftly, and with such strange pronunciations, that he was often misunderstood. But there was the time that Jackson was bragging about his IQ, and Rivers clearly said, "Reggie, you don't even know how to spell IQ." And Jackson's retort? "He said, 'You can't spell it, either.' Pretty lame."

Yesterday, Rivers testified to the fact that indeed he could spell IQ. "If you had a bad day, no matter who you were," Rivers said, "you got ripped."

Jackson signed as a free agent in the winter of 1976 after a lengthy romance by George Steinbrenner, the Yankees' principal owner. The Yankees had been swept in the World Series by the Reds that October, and Steinbrenner lusted for better.

The team had hardly begun spring training when Jackson announced he was "the straw that stirs the drink."

"Before this," Johnson said, "Thurman Munson was the man on this team, the player's player." Munson was the catcher and team leader, and resentment to Jackson came swiftly.

Johnson added, "For an outsider to come in and declare that, invading the territory, so to speak, rankled a lot of people. But Reggie thrived. He loved the attention, he loved the spotlight, the highlight, the lowlight, the flashlight—any light."

But as relief pitcher Sparky Lyle said, "He was the last piece of the puzzle. He was a hugely talented player on a very talented team."

Fran Healy, another backup catcher, said he had never seen anybody play under the intense pressure that Jackson did that season.

And Jackson agreed to a considerable extent. "There were a lot of expectations, a lot of demands, from teammates, from management, from ownership," Jackson said. "But I think I dealt with it okay."

Healy said, "The amazing thing about that team was that whatever was bothering the players, they didn't take it onto the field. And when the game was over, well, they just picked it up where they left off."

It was the emergence of Mr. October, the name bestowed by Steinbrenner after Jackson came through so handsomely in the World Series. In the sixth and deciding game of the Series against the Dodgers, Jackson hit his historic three consecutive home runs on three straight pitches from three different pitchers.

In a recent *New Yorker* article, it was related that "Steinbrenner still regards that night as his proudest moment in baseball—the moment he finally impressed his father."

Told this, Jackson said, "If that's the case, then I'm happy to have been a part of that."

Jackson had his battles with Steinbrenner, but it appears the two have reconciled any difficulties. "I told him I want to be his friend," Jackson said. "We have too much history behind us not to. We're tied together."

Jackson says today that he is "a wealthy man." He meant this in terms of happiness, of accomplishment, of health, and family. The plaque installed in Monument Park in his honor, he said, "is an honor up there with the Hall of Fame."

He added, "It's with the DiMaggios, the Ruths, the Gehrigs, and it's with the No. 1 franchise in sports in the No. 1 city in sports."

It was mentioned that Billy Martin has a plaque in the park as well. "I don't want to go into any ill feelings," Jackson said. "Let's just say I'm glad to be recognized."

Jackson said he also derived great satisfaction from the Reggie Jackson Foundation, which enhances educational opportunities for youths in the form of scholarships.

Looking back on that '77 team, Johnson said, "It was a wild ride, but worth taking because we achieved the ultimate."

In the mists of history and nostalgia, not all, but a great deal, is forgiven.

SOME OLD FACES
IN THE CLUBHOUSE

July 17, 1983

THE ELDERLY, BALDISH MAN in glasses and T-shirt stood in front of Rich Gossage's locker in Yankee Stadium yesterday and worked intently to pull the ends of a belt round the waist of his Yankee pin-striped knickers. He was Bill Johnson, a Yankee infielder in the 1940s and early 1950s, here for Old-Timers' Day. Beside him, sitting in front of George Frazier's locker, was Spud Chandler, the former pitcher who offered encouragement.

"You can make it, they'll stretch," said Chandler. "Ain't no way to stretch these belts," said Johnson, looking round the room like a man on a mountain in need of a St. Bernard. "I gotta find me a belt someplace."

"Hey, Pete," called Chandler, sizing up the situation. He got the attention of Pete Sheehy, the clubhouse man. "You got a belt for this guy?"

Some of the old-timers, like Chandler, managed to get into their uniforms easier than that, easier but slower. He wore No. 63. "I guess they thought they were giving me a number equal to my age," said Chandler. "I wish. I'm 76 years old."

One of the youngest old-timers was Catfish Hunter, 37, who still looked fit enough to pitch. In fact, he does. On Sundays, taking a day off from farming corn, soybeans, and peanuts in Hertford, North Carolina, he pitches occasionally for a local amateur team.

"I came in, in relief the last time and pitched nine innings in extra innings," he said. "We won 15–14." How did he do? "Well, one guy hit a homer off me," he said. How did it feel? "No different than when I was in the big leagues. I just looked at it." Ron Guidry walked over in street clothes and shook hands with Hunter, his onetime teammate. "Hey, Gator," said Hunter. "I see you're goin' less to the smoke." "You know how it is, Cat, when you get older, you gotta trick 'em," said Guidry. "I broke three bats up in Minnesota. I ain't never broke three bats before."

Hunter nodded. "I remember a water cooler once," he said. They laughed, as Hunter emptied some of the tobacco juice from his chaw into a wastebasket.

Ben Chapman removed the pipe from his mouth and walked over to Joe DiMaggio, who had just sat down in front of a locker. "First you take my job, now you take my locker," said Chapman.

DiMaggio looked up and began to rise, saying, "Is this your locker, Ben?" "Nah, I'm already dressed, go ahead, Joe," said Chapman. DiMaggio, white-haired, natty in a gray suit, blue shirt, and dark solid tie, sat back down. "And I never took your job," he said, smiling. "I came up as a left fielder. You were in center." "But not for long," said Chapman. It was in 1936. "I lasted a month out there, then they moved you to center," he recalled. "They traded me to Washington. Later Washington traded me to Boston, and I was playing left field when another rookie moved me out. That was Ted Williams. Talk about luck."

DiMaggio would suit up, but he wouldn't play. "My back gives me trouble," he said. He is 68. "And enough is enough," he added. "I played in my last old-timers' game when I was 60. But you can get hurt out there. I remember one year Earle Combs going after a fly ball, and his muscles tightened up and he had to be escorted off the field."

DiMaggio recalled his brief fling in left field. "I remember my first assist out there," he said. "It was against Detroit, in the ninth inning. We were ahead by one run with one out, and they had runners on first and third.

"A fly ball was hit down the foul line. The expected play after you catch the ball is to throw to second. You figure the run will score, and you try to keep the potential winning run from getting into scoring position. But I threw home on the fly, and Bill Dickey tagged out the runner, and it ended the game. I guess it was a daring throw. But you see, I knew myself, I knew that I had—well, I had a very strong arm, if I say so myself."

Dickey was in another corner of the room. He was a Yankee catcher for 17 years, and his hand, as one shakes it, is proof of his longevity behind the plate. "Every finger's been broken from foul tips," he said, "and you can see where the bones have come out of 'em."

Dickey, 75 and wearing a small hearing aid in his right ear, recalled his playing days. He said the best were the eight World Series he played in. "The saddest had to be losing Gehrig at such a young age," he said. "I was Lou's roommate for about nine or 10 years. I remember the morning of the afternoon he was going to take himself out of the lineup for the first time in 14 years. He was terribly sick, and we didn't know what it was. I remember that I used to always give him the ketchup bottle caps, and he opened them like they were nothing. Now, he handed me one, and it came off real easy." Gehrig set the record of 2,130 straight games, which still stands. [Cal Ripken Jr. broke the record in 1995.]

In another part of the clubhouse, Lefty Gomez, the former pitcher, was handed a baseball to sign. It was covered with signatures. "When you're goin' good," he said, "they always leave a nice space for you to sign a team ball. You know when you're on the way out when the only place for your autograph is on the seams."

Tommy Henrich, the onetime outfielder, walked by. "Lefty, you remember that day in Boston when I ran into the outfield wall after a drive that Williams hit, and I split open my head and they had to take me to the hospital?" he said.

Gomez nodded and said, "Of course I do. I was the pitcher."

"I was carried off the field on a stretcher and the fans in Fenway Park booed me!" said Henrich. "A couple innings before, I had bowled over their catcher at home plate. But still, they didn't know if I was dead or alive, and they were booing me."

"What I remember about that," said Gomez, "was that Joe McCarthy took me out of the game. Now, you're bleeding on the stretcher, and McCarthy looks around the dugout and says, 'We need somebody to go with Henrich to the hospital.' I was out of the game, so I said, 'I'll go.' McCarthy says, 'You! You nearly killed him!'"

On the other side of the clubhouse, Bill Johnson was in luck. He had found a belt for his pants. "Finally," he said. "It's tight as hell, but I guess it'll have to do."

HEALY'S GONE,
SO WHO'S ON FIRST NOW?

February 6, 1982

"SCOOTER," interrupted Fran Healy, the other commentator in the broadcasting booth, who had been listening to the story, "don't you think you ought to tell the people that the fly ball was caught?"

"Fly ball?" said Rizzuto. Rizzuto and Healy were a comedy team, one that also interspersed solid bits of baseball information that were a treat for Yankee fans. They rotated on the air with the other two Yankee announcers, Bill White and Frank Messer, but Rizzuto and Healy together had something special. They made people laugh—whether the anecdote was about Rizzuto's propensity to leave the game in the seventh inning to beat the traffic, or his experience when driving through Intercourse, Pennsylvania, a story that drove the producer to punch the "cough button" frantically, ending the travelogue.

Healy was Abbott to Rizzuto's Costello. The straight man and the laugh-getter. They insulted each other, they goaded each other, and they did so with warmth and, to a fair degree, good taste.

Philosophies emerged. One day they were talking about baseball today as opposed to the 1940s and '50s, when Rizzuto was a star shortstop for the Yankees.

"The game's more advanced today," said Healy, who retired as a Yankee catcher in 1978. "You've got a lot more coaching specialists. It's a lot more scientific."

"That's the problem," Rizzuto responded. "The game is supposed to be simple." Two weeks ago the team of Rizzuto and Healy was broken up.

Rizzuto was in an Italian restaurant on First Avenue when he heard the news. "A guy comes in," Rizzuto recalls, "and says, 'Hey, your buddy was just fired.' I said, 'What are you talking about?' He says, 'Fran Healy, they fired him.' I couldn't believe it."

Rizzuto left the table and phoned Art Adler, executive producer of Yankee radio broadcasting. "It's a big mistake," Rizzuto told Adler. "Is there anything I can do about it?"

Adler said he was sorry, but there wasn't. "I don't even feel like coming back next year without Fran in the booth," Rizzuto said the other day. "I never had so much fun in my life."

A number of the more than 2 million listeners of Yankee game broadcasts will miss Healy, too, and for the same reason. Subway riders, hanging onto vertical poles, were overheard quoting lines by Rizzuto and Healy from the night before. A cab driver was laughing so hard at their dialogue one night that his taxi ran up on a curb. In a letter of protest to Mr. Adler, Eric Levin, a devoted listener and a magazine editor, wrote, "They are the most delightful, madcap, and balanced broadcasting team in any sport. You'd have to go back to vaudeville to find their equal."

What happened? Why after four years was the curtain brought down on this obviously successful act? "It was great improvisational radio," said Mr. Adler, "but we needed more than that from Fran." It seems that doing play-by-play as opposed to color commentary was, to his superiors, a weak point of Healy's. "If it was a deficiency, it never bothered me," said Mr. Levin. "I always thought I got the picture of the game." Another question was raised by Rizzuto. "It seems more than a coincidence that Fran was fired at about the same time that Reggie Jackson left the Yankees."

Healy is a close friend of Jackson's, and, during Jackson's turbulent years in New York, Healy was often one of the few people to whom Jackson would confide.

Healy, unlike the three other Yankee announcers, was employed directly by the Yankees instead of by a radio or TV station. Jackson and George Steinbrenner, the Yankee owner, did not always see eye to eye. Was Healy being punished now for being friendly to Jackson?

"It would be unfair to both George and Reggie to project that," said Healy. "Anyway, I tend to doubt it." Steinbrenner said, "I listened to about 60 percent of the games on the radio from my home in Tampa, and sometimes Fran and Phil talked about everything but baseball—to the detriment of the game. But the reasons for dropping Fran were strictly Art Adler's. He makes the decisions on talent for radio."

Steinbrenner added that "sometimes you have to make moves that aren't always popular." With Rizzuto getting near retirement—he's 63—and Messer not far behind in age, it is believed that the Yankee radio officials want to groom another announcer to take over more play-by-play responsibilities, and that meant the ax for Healy.

One other point about Healy. Pleasant, disarmingly curious, with a good eye for baseball detail and technique, he demonstrated the ability, rare among sports broadcasters, to draw out guests with questions. His postgame show was exceptional in this regard. Near the end of the 1980 season, he asked Tommy John—a 22-game winner for the Yankees' Eastern Division champions—who he thought might win the Cy Young Award, and whether Steve Stone of the Orioles should.

"Stone had a good year," responded John. "He managed to pitch his team into second place." That's the kind of stuff that Yankee radio fans will miss without Fran Healy around. After all, man does not live by play-by-play alone.

YESTERDAY WAS JUST PERFECT FOR A BALLGAME

August 29, 1994

YANKEE STADIUM was like a morgue yesterday. The sun was shining brightly, the field was gorgeous with the manicured grass as green as a pool table, the tan infield dirt was smartly raked. It was a perfect day for a ballgame. The first-place Yankees, according to the schedule, were supposed to be playing the Texas Rangers, in the heat of a pennant race. But Yankee Stadium yesterday was as silent as a cadaver.

Except for the soft whir of the sprinkler system that is run by computers in the stadium basement and which pop up for a time first in right field, and then behind third base, and somewhere else after that, the playing field, the broad, wondrous, sweeping diamond, was empty. No runners, no hitters, no one to err.

Like the stands. Like all of the 57,545 stark blue seats in the ballpark. From the box seats to the grandstands to the bleachers that curve down from the familiar Gothic façade of the roof. Empty. No cheering. No booing. Nothing.

If someone had been held captive in a cave for the last few weeks and was released to see a ballgame here and didn't know anything about the strike—the dispute between the major league owners and the players that is now in its 18th day—he might have wondered: Have I arrived too late and the game is over? After all, cigarette butts remain in the aisles, and peanut shells, and flattened paper

cups. Or maybe there had been a bomb scare, and everyone evac-
uated. Surely something weird had occurred.

It was reminiscent of a recurring dream that Mickey Mantle had
shortly after his retirement. He dreamed of going to a game and
not being allowed in. That there were locks on the gates. And he
heard his name announced as the next batter. It was a sad dream.
A kind of nightmare. For baseball fans now, this, too, is a bad
dream come true.

No one there to buy a hot dog that is advertised on a sign in the
grandstand. No one to hail a vendor for a Slurpee, as seen on
another sign in the outfield. There was no crack of the bat. No
smack of a fastball into the catcher's plump mitt. No one to stretch
in the seventh and wail, "Take Me Out to the Ballgame."

The skeleton crew in the Yankee office was off yesterday. The
space in the parking lot reserved for George Steinbrenner's limou-
sine, and those for the cars of his pinstriped employees, was vacant.
Only a couple of security men and an engineer were on the premises, to keep things in working order in case someone turned the
season back on.

Across the street from the ballpark and under the elevated train
tracks on River Road, Stan's Sports Bar and Grill is shuttered
down. Discount Dugout is closed. As is Baseball Land. Only Stadium Souvenir is open, but the proprietor, Abdul Al Sacahi, says
business is dead.

"Very slow, they wreck my business," he said, as a train rumbled
overhead. He held up a slip of paper. "Here, this is my bill for the
rent. $4,500. I can't pay it. Maybe have to close up next week. They
told me they don't know when strike will be over. They told me
maybe next month. Maybe next year. Have you heard anything?"

No one knows, unless it's the owners. And they are gagging
themselves.

On the other side of Yankee Stadium is Macombs Dam Park,
with a sign above a handball court that reads, "We Do Care. New
York Yankees Neighborhood Project 2." There is also a basketball
court and a ballfield. Games were on both.

The basketball court was a center of controversy earlier in the
season when Richard Kraft, the Yankees' vice president in charge

of community relations, was forced to resign after supposedly telling a magazine reporter that kids hung "like monkeys" from the rims.

"Most of us don't try to hang from the rims," said Abe Johnson, one of the Sunday morning players, who works in computers for Smith Barney. "We like the rims straight. But maybe one or two of the younger kids was trying to imitate the pros."

How did he feel about the major league situation? "Baseball is commercialism," said Johnson. "And I think there's greed on both sides. But I majored in economics, and I know it's likely that the owners have two sets of books."

At the ballfield, there was, unlike the big white structure across the road, a ballgame in progress. It was a kids' game between the green-and-white-uniformed Rosado Design team and the red-and-white NatWest nine.

"I told you to swing only at strikes, Irvin," said a coach to a player.

"It was a strike," said the player.

"It almost hit you in the head—how can you call that a strike?" said the coach.

Another hitter lined a single. "Way to rip, Jacob!" came a shout from the bleachers.

The players were playing on a field with grass up to their ankles. A Stadium groundskeeper could have done wonders in minutes.

"It's a shame," said Dennis Centeno, the NatWest coach. "One of my kids could get hurt because you can't see the holes in the field."

It was a hot day under the sun. There were two water fountains nearby, but both were broken. "My players are thirsty, and there's nothing to drink, so I have to run to the store to buy them juice," said Centeno. "I know the Yankees have a sign that says they care. But how much?"

One player wondered if any Yankees were in the park. "What's wrong with you?" said a teammate. "Do you think they're playing dominoes? It's a strike!"

Some around the Stadium thought the owners right, some the players. Like some editorial writers, some thought neither was right. But if, in America, one side, the players, are seeking only to maintain their position of being paid for what they can command in the open market, what's so wrong?

In Yankee Stadium now, the water fountain in the dugout was dusty. The railings in the vacant stands sparkled in the sunlight. But all that bespoke of baseball were the silent monuments in center field. The ghosts of Ruth and Gehrig and DiMaggio and Mantle.

It was a perfect day for a ballgame. But all was still. Like a morgue.

BASEBALL SEASON: NO TRESPASSING

August 3, 1987

OVER THE WEEKEND, a horde of helmeted behemoths invaded the landscape. They are known as football players, and they began that preternatural ritual called "training camp," right here, right in the midst of the American summertime, right in the thick of its baseball season.

History records other hordes that invaded other terrains, such as the Goths, the Visigoths, the Ostrogoths, and, perhaps a primeval ancestor of these modern behemoths, moths themselves.

Don't laugh about moths. They are "distinguished from butterflies," the *New Columbia Encyclopedia* informs us, by their "stouter, usually hairy body...." Precisely like football players.

If you still think the analogy between a moth and a behemoth is farfetched, consider the following:

It is widely known that moths prefer an unusual type of cuisine—clothes, with sweaters as the single most popular entrée.

Football players have been known to consume huge helpings of anything. Note the recent remark by the coach of the Bears, who, when told that William Perry has been doing a lot of running in the off-season, said, "Running where? From the refrigerator to the bathroom?"

But football behemoths, like the bee moths, are closer to gourmands than gourmets in their dining habits.

A case in point is that engaging fellow from the Giants, Lawrence Taylor. In his recently released and widely discussed opus, *LT*, he describes an incident in college when he was drinking beer with some other athletes, and one of them "drank down his beer, and then made a point of just breaking the glass. All the guys got off on that. What I did was to then take another glass, break it on the side of the bar, and then begin eating it."

LT is an amiable bloke whose greatest joy in life besides eating glass, it seems, is to snarl and to jump on someone and hear that fellow's bones snap.

Thus it is with football players overall. To be sure, football has its moments. But they ought not to be during this time of the calendar year. It is a brutal sport, a sullen sport, and perfect for the miseries of winter. The participants crash into each another and pile one on top of the other, and it serves a necessary purpose: it keeps them warm.

But now it is baseball, gentlemen and gentlewomen, baseball. We have these pennant races to consider, and they are just heating up. We have box scores to peruse, and standings to analyze and miles to go before we sleep. We have no time for football. If the helmeted behemoths must go charging into blocking dummies, and knocking heads, and sacking QBs, let them do it underground, or in caves, from whence they came lo those many epochs ago.

We have batting races to observe, and pitching performances to chart, and managerial machinations to monitor.

In some ways, this role model for something, LT, is unintentionally doing us all a favor by not deigning to offer the pearls of his considerable wisdom to the press. He is not talking to scribes.

Neither, at times, has Brian Bosworth, a man of deepest intellect and the only athlete in history who appears to comb his hair with Crayolas.

In the middle of all this comes a baseball player who says baseball is not enough for him. He needs a hobby. Needlepoint? Hang gliding? Building sand castles? Not on your life. Bo Jackson says football. And he goes ahead and negotiates with the Raiders, a perfect name, it happens, for a successor to the Visigoths, the Ostrogoths, or the bee moths.

Jackson's decision disturbed his teammates, disgruntled the Kansas City fans, and put baseball followers generally into a modicum of a funk.

But the national pastime is resilient. And fans return to the thrill of the pennant scrambles, and the redheaded rookie McGwire as he pursues Maris and 61, and the red-bearded veteran Boggs as he chases Williams and .406.

The mention of Williams recalls a moment last Monday that underscores a point. Williams was encountered at Cooperstown, that pastoral town where Abner Doubleday did not invent baseball but where he ought to have. Williams had attended the induction ceremony there of three new members to the Baseball Hall of Fame.

On the field before the exhibition game between the Yankees and the Braves, a man walked over to Williams. "Hello, Ted, my name's Bobby Murcer." "Oh, hello," said Williams, politely. Suddenly the name sunk in. "Bobby Murcer! How are you!"

Murcer said, "Ted, there's something I have wanted to ask you for a long time." "Sure, what is it, Bobby?" Murcer then recalled a time in the early 1970s when he was playing with the Yankees and Williams was managing the Senators and later, the Rangers.

"You stood behind the batting cage one day and said, 'Murcer, you've got a beautiful swing, but you've got one small flaw.' I asked you what it was, and you said you'd tell me after the season, because if you told me then I might beat your team with a base hit." Williams nodded. "Well," Murcer continued. "I missed you at the end of the season. The next season, the same thing happened, and you said you'd tell me at the end of that year. I missed you again, and you retired. For the last 16 years I've been dying to find out, what was that small flaw in my swing?"

"You know, Bobby," said Williams, "it's been so long, I don't remember anymore."

In the American summertime, baseball games and baseball lore should not brook intruders.

There is plenty of time for football when the winds howl and the snow comes.

DOWN BROADWAY

October 31, 2000

NEITHER SNOW (blizzards of confetti), nor heat (a sanitation truck caught fire), nor chill (mid-40s with a stinging wind), nor inconveniences (a paucity of portable toilets), nor school (thousands of truants roamed lower Broadway after the mayor virtually sanctioned the unlocking of classrooms), nor yet another victory parade for the New York Yankees could stay these throngs of fans from the sweet contemplation of their appointed heroes.

One might imagine that these wild and crazy fans would get bored with the whole thing—this fourth World Series championship parade in five years. You might think they'd be smarter (we're told often enough, after all, that this is the mecca of the streetwise, the hipster, the coolest cats) than wallowing in crowds, flinging ever more paper, jumping up and down at the sight a bunch of young men dressed in what was primarily the mode of the day: leather jackets, jeans, sunglasses (most of them, though, generally recognizable away from the ballpark even without, as Michelle Wernert-Piper, a Frenchwoman recent to these shores, observed, "those funny costumes").

But no, these wild and crazy fans do not get bored with it all, because they are wild and crazy. Such comportment is given full rein in the Fans' Bill of Rights. And so after the floats had taken the players and the manager and the owner and all the rest of the Yankee entourage to the steps of City Hall, the fans, amid blue and white balloons and big banners and bunting festooning the building, were shaking pom-poms and screaming at the top of their lungs.

Mayor Rudolph W. Giuliani, wearing a Yankee cap, to be sure, handed out keys to the city to the Yankees. He is an ardent fan and applauded when one of the Yankee announcers, Michael Kay, introduced this team as "maybe the best team in baseball history," given that they've won three straight World Series and had to do it in the rugged playoff system that didn't begin until some 30 years ago.

This Yankee team has at least three potential Hall of Famers: Derek Jeter, Roger Clemens, and Mariano Rivera. A perennial All-Star in Bernie Williams. And a passel of excellent veteran players—from Tino to O'Neill to Pettitte—who know how to win. They beat everybody they had to beat. But might other teams, and other Yankee teams—the DiMaggio, Raschi, Reynolds, and Yogi Berra teams of the '40s and '50s, which won five World Series in a row, for one; the Mantle, Maris, Ford, and Berra teams of the early '60s, for another—have been better?

When the point about the 2000 Yankees was raised by Kay yesterday, Berra, seated on the podium in a gray topcoat, smiled, but only politely. The man of many words—not all of them always in syntactical order—didn't have to say anything else.

But New Yorkers can take ample pride in this team of people from regions as far-flung as Texas and Michigan and Ohio and Puerto Rico and Panama and Brooklyn. The spirit was a generous one at the ceremony, with Giuliani praising the Mets, who had been defeated in the Subway Series, and asking Yankee fans for a cheer for the Mets. The fans indeed responded with one (but only one).

Several players spoke, like Jeter expressing appreciation to the fans and admiration for his teammates. David Cone, who may be at the end of his Yankee career after a difficult season, said how glad he was to be there, and added poignantly, "I may never get this chance again."

Then Jorge Posada, the catcher, and Orlando "El Duque" Hernandez, the gritty Cuban pitcher, were called to the microphone. El Duque, who is known to speak only Spanish, took the microphone. He whispered something to Posada, who nodded. "He wants to talk to you in English," Posada told the crowd. El Duque cleared his throat. "I feel very well," he said before twice saying thank you. El Duque smiled shyly. Everyone broke up. The fans cheered.

"He should take that on Broadway," said George Steinbrenner, the Yankee principal owner. The event ended with balloons released into the cool blue sky, and the organist striking up "New York, New York."

"Wait till next year," someone in the crowd said. Was he talking about a fourth straight Yankee world championship? Not likely. He was wearing, of all things, a Mets cap.

VI.

A Handful of
Notable Rivals

COOKIE LAVAGETTO'S DOUBLE

August 13, 1990

COOKIE LAVAGETTO, who died at age 77 in his sleep Friday morning at his home in Orinda, California, was famous for one thing: he was the Brooklyn Dodger who struck a celebrated pinch-hit in the 1947 World Series. Thoughts of Lavagetto the ballplayer led to the notion here that great moments in sports don't last as long as they used to.

The reason, I decided at first, was me. The older I become, the quicker life goes. More events are stuffed into a shrinking time frame. In the grade-school years, a summer vacation lasted forever. Now, a summer zips by nearly like a weekend. Yesterday it was July. Tomorrow it's September. Yesterday, Cookie Lavagetto was batting against Floyd Bevens of the Yankees at Ebbets Field with two out in the bottom half of the ninth inning of the fourth game of the Series. Bevens had a no-hitter going. Just one more out. There had never been a no-hitter thrown in the 43 previous World Series. There were two runners on, by virtue of walks, the ninth and 10th that Bevens had given up in the game. Because of his wildness, Bevens had allowed a run in the fifth inning, but he was still ahead 2–1.

Lavagetto was 34 years old and a 10-year big-league veteran when summoned by Manager Burt Shotton to pinch-hit for Eddie Stanky. The capacity crowd of 33,443 was on its feet. Lavagetto swung and missed at the first pitch, and then hit the next pitch off the top of the right-field wall, breaking up Bevens' no-hitter, driving in the two runs, and giving the Dodgers a 3–2 victory.

Brooklyn erupted. Lavagetto was pummeled by his teammates. Fans and vendors pummeled one another. In his book *1947— When All Hell Broke Loose in Baseball*, Red Barber recalled announcing the game on radio, which dwarfed the television coverage, because it was the first televised World Series, and seen only on the Eastern Seaboard.

"I remember the final sentence I said," Barber wrote. It was: "I'll be a suck-egg mule." I was a boy when all this was going on, although I don't remember the game or the broadcast. What I remember is that the Lavagetto hit, the Bevens failed no-hitter, and the sensational catch by Al Gionfriddo to rob Joe DiMaggio of a home run in that Series all became part of the lore of baseball for me, the lore of America, as famous as anything Paul Bunyan did, or Tom Sawyer, or even George Washington.

There are still a lot of great achievements going on all over the place these days in sports, but somehow they fail to stick in the brain as they once did.

Who won Wimbledon last year, or this? Who won the Super Bowl three years ago? Who'd they beat? If not for the earth rhumba in California last year, some of us would hardly remember the 1989 World Series. Who was the MVP, anyway?

The reason is not old age, or amnesia, necessarily; it's the glut of events, brought on in no small part by the voracity of television.

There are so many more sports and players to be involved with, from coverage of the World Cup to professional volleyball to tractor pulls, and so many more teams: there are 10 more Major League Baseball teams than the 16 in 1947; nearly three times as many National Football League teams (28 teams now); more than three times as many National Basketball Association teams (25 teams); three and a half times as many National Hockey League teams (21 teams), and maybe quadruple the boxing champions.

And so many more big events, so much more overlapping of seasons, and a preponderance of playoffs.

And there are so many milestones to contend with. Rose's breaking Cobb's career hit mark—a record that had seemed secure for the ages—is one thing, or perhaps even Nolan Ryan's 300th victory at 43 when Ryan is still throwing a fastball at locomotive speed, but every time you look up at the scoreboard, someone else is getting his 50th hit in the major leagues, making his 25th double play, or committing his 10th balk. There seems no surcease to the mind-numbing march of numbers.

Nutrition might be partly to blame, too. Players are lasting longer, thus getting thicker stats, and probably because a greater number of them are spending more time with Wheaties than with John Barleycorn. Once, great moments seemed to last longer. Fred Merkle's bonehead play in 1908, Ruth's supposedly called home run in the '32 Series, Dizzy Dean's Gashouse feats in the '34 Series remain a vivid part of our national heritage.

There were, too, no instant replays, nor the continual replays on the evening news of all those moments. Today, everything is a sound bite or a visual bite. Once, there was only a picture in a newspaper or a book. Or the description on the radio. And the imagination did the rest. The special moment hung like a painting in the mind's eye, and for all time.

Perhaps, too, that was a simpler time, when the world wasn't so crowded and close, and America was like a small town. "Come out and smell the heliotrope in the moonlight," Mrs. Gibbs said to her husband in Thornton Wilder's *Our Town*. For some of us, it was a little like that.

We had time to savor our exceptional moments, to smell the heliotrope in the moonlight, to ruminate on Lavagetto's double. And even to remember the bittersweet ironies of something like the 1947 World Series. Neither Gionfriddo, Bevens, nor Lavagetto ever played another season in the major leagues.

KOUFAX IS NO GARBO

July 3, 1985

WASHINGTON, D.C. — There was something special about Sandy Koufax. On Monday night, in the Cracker Jack Old-Timers' Baseball Classic at Robert F. Kennedy Stadium here, he was chosen as the honorary captain of the National League team, a singular plum among such teammates as Henry Aaron and Ernie Banks and Warren Spahn. Koufax retains that special quality, apparently, even among his peers.

Perhaps it has something to do with an almost Biblical cycle to his baseball career. Koufax didn't quite have seven years thin and ill-favored, and seven years of great plenty, but he did have six of each.

Miraculously, it seemed, he went from a pitcher of enormous but uncontrolled potential—catchers wore shin-guards when warming him up because so many of his pitches bounced in the dirt in front of them—to a star of the greatest mastery.

"What was it like facing Koufax? It was frightenin'," Banks, the former star Cub, recalled at the Cracker Jack, which the National League won 7–3. "He had that tremendous fastball that would rise, and a great curveball that started at the eyes and broke to the ankles. In the end, you knew you were going to be embarrassed. You were either going to strike out or foul out."

Koufax's record was 36–40 in his first six seasons, 129–47 in his last six.

Maybe that special quality of Koufax also had to do with his poise and grit on the mound: the memory remains vivid of his breaking a World Series record in 1963 by striking out 15 Yankees in a game. Maybe the special quality also was enhanced by the air of distinction with which he comported himself, even to the way he adjusted his cap front and back, with two fingers of each hand, like knotting a bow tie.

And maybe the quality also had something to do with the way he retired, at the young age of 30, after having been named the Cy Young Award winner in 1966 for the third time in four years, after having led the major leagues in victories with 27, and earned run average, 1.73, and games started and games completed and innings pitched and strikeouts, with 317, and after having helped pitch the Los Angeles Dodgers to a pennant, their second straight.

He suffered from an arthritic elbow, and doctors feared that if he continued pitching he could cause permanent damage to his arm.

And so, virtually at the height of his career, Koufax retired. And moved to a small town in Maine. Here was the toast of New York and Los Angeles departing the bright lights for what seemed to some the life of Greta Garbo.

To some, he became a kind of mystery man.

"What was so mysterious?" he asked, dressing for the game in the Cracker Jack clubhouse. "I wasn't running away, or hiding from the police. Maine is not another world. A lot of people lived there, and still do."

He said yes, he sought some privacy. "I never liked being shoved and pushed in crowds," he said. "But I was around for six years doing Saturday afternoon baseball telecasts with NBC.

"And now I work for the Dodgers. I'm a pitching coach with the team in spring training and a minor league pitching instructor during the summer months. I'm around. What's the mystery?"

Red Schoendienst came by. "Sandy," he said, "looks like you can go out there and still pump the heat."

Koufax smiled. At 6', 185 pounds, he does look fit. He was tan and slim and perhaps only the hair on his head, more salt than pepper now, gives an indication that on his next birthday, December 30, he will be 50 years old.

He spoke about traveling as a pitching instructor and working with young players. Bill Schweppe, the Dodgers' vice president in charge of minor league operations, said that Koufax was effective with kids once they got past their awe of him. He mentioned Koufax's low-key approach that puts players at ease.

"In the minor leagues, the players are on the way up and they've all got their dreams," said Koufax. "It's a very positive thing. They want to learn. But I don't know how much I've helped anyone. I can show them some mechanics, but no one can make a big-league ballplayer. In the end it's up to the individual. They help themselves. But it's satisfying to see improvement."

He had said that he became a better pitcher when he learned to control his temper and his frustration. "Maybe it was just a matter of getting older," he said. "I see young players getting angry with themselves the way I did, and I wish I could tell them how to curb it. But there's no secret formula."

Koufax grew up in Brooklyn, joined the Dodgers there in 1955, at age 19, and never played a day in the minor leagues. "If I walked five guys in a major league game, it was terrible," he said, "but if I had done that in the minors, where I should have been, it would have been fine—a learning experience."

He contends that there was no single turning point. "I had a good spring in 1961," he said, "and it seemed that management was finally going to let me pitch every fourth day. Before, if I didn't do well in an outing, I might not pitch for three weeks. That didn't help me. I kept telling the Dodgers that I needed a routine. Your control is dependent on consistency."

In his younger, more inept days, a story goes that Koufax, who is Jewish, said he wasn't sure whether he was a shlemiel or a shlamazel. In Yiddish, a shlemiel is someone who spills soup on people, a shlamazel is someone who has soup spilled on him.

"Or is it vice versa?" Koufax said smiling. "I really don't remember if I ever said that, but there were times when I felt that way."

As he spoke, a television crew came by and began shooting him from the side. The bright light made him blink. He turned to the three men. "Don't television people ever ask?" he said, with a half smile.

"I'm sorry," said the man who apparently was head of the crew. He introduced himself. Koufax shook his hand, and said, "At least let me put on my shirt before you continue."

Later, he was asked if he still goes back to Maine. "Every year," he said. "I still love it."

SEAVER: A FAMILY AFFAIR

August 5, 1985

THE DAY BEGAN with a bat in Tom Seaver's bedroom. Not a Louisville Slugger, but an airborne mammal who had found his way through a window into the Seaver family's house in Greenwich, Connecticut.

It was about 5:30 yesterday morning when Seaver and his wife, Nancy, were awakened. They jumped out of bed and flung their arms, grabbed a broom, and gave other appropriate signals to the intruder that he was not wanted, especially at this hour, and especially on this day.

The bat finally took the hint and winged off. The Seavers returned to bed, to continue perchance the dream of what he called "the storybook touch."

This was the fitful morning before the memorable afternoon in which George Thomas Seaver would attempt to earn his 300th victory as a major league pitcher. He was pitching for Chicago, but he was back in New York, where he began his major league career 19 years ago and where, it seems, his heart is.

Seaver has had two stretches with the Mets. Each time he left, he did so with heavy heart. He has maintained his residence in the metropolitan area.

The victory would make Seaver only the 17th pitcher in baseball history to win 300 games. He is among the career leaders in earned-run average and strikeouts and class, and if he doesn't get elected

214

to the Hall of Fame on the first ballot, there are some fans who might justifiably call for a Congressional investigation.

Looking well-rested despite his bout with the bat, Seaver was in the White Sox clubhouse at Yankee Stadium later that morning, answering questions from reporters, accepting congratulations from the White Sox owners Jerry Reinsdorf and Eddie Einhorn, and autographing some baseballs.

"This one," said a clubhouse man, "is from Rickey Henderson." Seaver, seated on a stool before his locker, looked up.

"No kidding," said the clubhouse man. "He gave me the ball for you to sign."

At 2:09 PM, Seaver came out of the dugout to walk across the field and headed for the bullpen in left-center to warm up for the game. Fans in the area cheered. They were cheering an opponent, yes, but they were cheering a man who for 11½ years had been one of the most popular and accomplished athletes in New York history.

As a pitcher with the Mets, he won three Cy Young Awards and helped pitch them to two pennants and one World Series victory.

Despite a list of exceptional days in his career, this was special, and there was no disguising that. So special that he had his father, Charles Seaver, and his father-in-law, Dean McIntyre, fly in from California for the game, to join Nancy and their two children, Sarah (14) and Annie (nine).

The crowd of 54,032 noisily greeted Seaver as he came out to pitch the first inning against the Yankees. "My head hurt, I was so nervous," Seaver would recall. "I talked myself into its being just another game, but deep down you know it's not just another game."

Most of the fans cheered, but there was a smattering of boos. "I can't believe all the Met fans out there screaming for Chicago," said a Yankee fan in the stands.

He would have been closer to the fact if he had said "baseball fans."

The category "Seaver fan" was well-represented, too, of course, and no better constituents exist than the five seated immediately to the right of the White Sox dugout, the four Seavers and the McIntyre.

Seaver's first pitch of the game, a strike to Henderson, was greeted with appreciative applause from his daughters. Nancy, though, leaned forward and held onto the top of the low wall in front of her. After 21 years of marriage to a hurler, she understands that one pitch does not a game make.

Under generally clear skies and a warm sun, they cheered when the White Sox threatened to score in the first, the second, the third, the fourth, and the fifth innings, but came up empty each time.

Annie held her White Sox cap with two hands, and Sarah sat with her head resting in the palm of her hand when the Yankees scored a run off Pop in the third.

The Seaver contingent was on its feet when the Sox scored four runs in the sixth to give the old man a thick cushion on which to work.

It was an ambivalent crowd. It cheered the Yanks when they had scoring opportunities, but they booed the White Sox pitching coach, Dave Duncan, when he walked out to the mound in the eighth to talk to Seaver. With two on and two out, the dangerous Dave Winfield was coming to the plate. The crowd didn't want Seaver removed. And he wasn't.

The count ran to 3–2 on Winfield. Seaver, partly in the Stadium shadows now, wound up and fired home, following through in that long, low, familiar stride.

Winfield swung and missed mightily to end the inning. The crowd roared, and the five in the Seaver group leaped to their feet in exultation.

The old man calmly walked off the mound, seemingly cool as could be, the unexcitable professional, but, surely, as happy and relieved as his kin.

Now, in the Yankee ninth, he would just finish off the next three batters.

But not so fast. Dan Pasqua, the Yankees' first hitter, lined a single off the right-field wall. Seaver struck out the next batter, but Willie Randolph followed with a smash that Harold Baines grabbed when he crashed into the right-field wall. Another White Sox conference on the mound.

"I was beat as hell," Seaver would recall, "but there wasn't a chance in hell I was coming out, not on this day." He stayed. But the tired Seaver walked Mike Pagliarulo.

Now Don Baylor batted for Bobby Meacham. The formidable Baylor represented the tying run with the score 4–1. He swung hard and lofted a high fly to left field. Reid Nichols came in, then went back.

And Nichols had it. And so did Seaver. No. 300 was his.

As his White Sox teammates hurried over to congratulate him, Seaver headed for his family. He hugged his wife, the girls, and his father and father-in-law.

Meanwhile, most of the fans had not left the park and they stood, some with tears, and continued to clap.

Yesterday, for that one day, anyway, most of the people at Yankee Stadium felt just like the five in the first row, like family.

MADDUX: A BASEBALL PICASSO

June 23, 1998

GREG MADDUX is an artist," Joe Torre, the Yankee manager, has said. "Every time you swing at one of his pitches, it's a ball, and when you don't, it's a strike."

Indeed, Maddux, the Atlanta Braves right-hander, permits so little activity on the bases that each game he pitches could be titled *Still Life*.

Not last night, however. The canvas got a little crowded for him at Yankee Stadium, in the first game of a series that has been billed as a possible preview of the World Series. Maddux allowed nine hits and three runs before departing after six innings with a 4–3 lead, and he learned from the showers that the Yankees had won 6–4, with no-decision for him.

It was less than one of his routine masterpieces—even Picasso had the occasional bungle—but when Maddux had to be dazzling, he was. In the sixth inning, with two runners on base and one out in a 3–3 game, he struck out Scott Brosius and forced Joe Girardi to bounce weakly to the mound.

Maddux then left the game, having been plagued by a stiff neck he had awakened with and which troubled him so much that he almost didn't start. "It was killing him," Braves manager Bobby Cox said.

Maddux won the Cy Young Award four straight years (1992–1995) and is the leading pitcher in the National League again, with a 10–2 record—he has won eight in a row—and a 1.62 earned-run average. And he has achieved his mastery so effortlessly that it's mystifying.

Mark Grace, the Chicago Cubs' first baseman, observed that Maddux pitches "like he's in a rocking chair." Like Grandma Moses?

"I know absolutely nothing about art," Maddux said last weekend. "If there was an art handicap like there is a golf handicap, I would be a 50."

What, then, is the esthetic secret to his success, which is certain to land him in the Hall of Fame? Now in his 13th major league season, Maddux has nearly twice as many victories, 194, as losses, 110, and his strikeout-to-walk ratio is also remarkable; last year, he gave up just 20 walks while striking out 177 batters. Last night, he whiffed four and walked none.

There is nothing outwardly noteworthy about perhaps the best pitcher of our time. He has the demeanor of a bookkeeper. He is 32 years old, stands 6' tall, weighs 175 pounds. He wears glasses off the field, has a physique that would not draw attention at the beach, rarely shows emotion, and frustrates batters to such a degree that they nearly weep.

Some pitchers throw the ball at nearly 100 mph, some have wicked breaking balls. Maddux has neither. "I saw Sandy Koufax and I saw Nolan Ryan," he said, "and I knew I couldn't pitch like those guys. I wasn't going to overpower anybody."

His fastball is generally clocked in the mid- to upper 80s, and he uses breaking balls sparingly. "I found that velocity can be misleading," he said. "I rely on location of my fastball and on change-ups. If you stand by a highway and watch cars go by, you can't really tell which one is going 80 miles an hour and which is going 90. And if you throw real hard every pitch, hitters will eventually time them."

Maddux learned from other masters of the mound. His classroom was the dugout. When he studied Mario Soto, he discerned that one could win with, basically, two pitches. "Soto was able to pitch effectively with just a fastball and a change-up," Maddux said. "Which is what I do—though his fastball was better than mine. You locate your fastball, and you keep your change-up down. If that doesn't work, you'll be backing up third and home all day."

Unlike many in sports who analyze and parse and dissect and deconstruct the commonplace components of running, jumping, and hurling, Maddux wants no part of it. "You do something well in sports, it gets magnified," he said. "I just throw a baseball for a living."

His consistency, his professionalism, and his understanding of hitters and of his own abilities, however, belie such a casual approach.

"I try to keep it simple," he said. "At the same time, I try not to be too smart. The fewest amount of pitches you throw a hitter, the greater your chances of getting him out."

Then a crucial element of success for Maddux is that less is more. "In art," Henry James wrote, "economy is always beauty." Not in the eye of every beholder. For batters who must swing at pitches on their fists, or at their knees, or in the crevices of the strike zone where they are least likely to do damage, it is ugly. A tapper here, a pop fly there, a lunge for strike three. Ask Brosius or Girardi, among others. Modern art, one could almost hear a batter mutter. It stinks.

MANNY RAMIREZ: FORMIDABLE, AND FORGETFUL

September 23, 1997

IN ONE GAME earlier this season Manny Ramirez was thrown out trying to steal first base. The youthful Cleveland right fielder, by way of Washington Heights and George Washington High School in upper Manhattan, had stolen second base, then looked around, and trotted back to first. The pitcher, blinking to make sure he was seeing correctly, tossed the ball to the second baseman, who tagged Ramirez out.

In his typically noncommittal way, the bill of his baseball cap tugged low on his head to shadow his eyes, Ramirez then trotted to the dugout.

"Sometimes," said John Hart, the Indians' general manager, "Manny has concentration lapses."

The Cleveland manager, Mike Hargrove, did not immediately discuss the play with his erstwhile base runner.

"I had never seen anything like it in all my years in baseball," Hargrove said, "but I didn't go over right away and talk to Manny. I was so mad I would have killed him. I waited for the next inning."

The following inning, Ramirez explained to Hargrove that he thought there was a foul ball and was simply returning to first base. "Never leave a base without asking the umpire, 'Can I leave?'" Hargrove said slowly, perhaps restraining any homicidal urge. "Okay?"

"Okay," replied the player.

Off the field, Ramirez has got himself into strange situations, as well. Like his driving. He was recently stopped while driving his black Mercedes and given three tickets—one for windows tinted too dark, one for playing music too loud, and one for an illegal driver's license. When Ramirez got back into his car, he nodded good-bye to the police officer and proceeded to make a U-turn. Ticket No. 4.

Ramirez is in his fourth full season in the major leagues, having come up to the Indians in September 1993, and has been in the lineup virtually from the moment he arrived.

Now, at age 25, and despite various problems of focus and maturity, he has become one of baseball's best hitters, one who hits for power and for average. Entering last night's games—the Indians' game in Kansas City was rained out—he was batting .331, tied for second in the American League, with 25 homers and 84 runs batted in. He was 10th in slugging percentage (.539), sixth in on-base percentage (.420), and fifth in hits (179).

And he will be a formidable presence not only when the Indians face the Yankees today at Yankee Stadium, but also in the likely first-round playoff matchup between the two teams in the next week.

He was in right field when the Indians lost to the Braves in the 1995 World Series and was selected that year for the American League All-Star team. In the last two seasons, respectively, he has hit .308 and .309, with 31 and 33 homers and 107 and 112 RBIs.

And his hits have been important in many ways for the Indians this season.

In early September against the White Sox, a challenger of the Indians in the Central Division, the well-built, 6', 190-pound Ramirez whacked a prodigious homer with runners on base to clinch a victory and help knock Chicago out of the running. Last Monday against the Orioles, he niftily put his bat on a pitch low and away and knocked it into right field for a double, scoring two big runs in the Indians' victory.

"He's one of the few players I let swing with a 3–0 count," Hargrove said. "And he doesn't swing wildly. If it's a ball, he lets it pass. A lot of young players wouldn't."

Hitting is by far the best part of Ramirez's game. "He's improved in the other areas, too," Hargrove said, "but he's still got a way to go."

Sometimes he has walked on three pitches, only to be reminded by the umpire to return to the plate from first base. Sometimes it has to be suggested to him to leave home plate after ball four has been thrown.

Against Houston this season, a ball was hit under the bullpen bench and Ramirez threw up his hands as if to say he couldn't get it. But the ground rules stipulated that they had to dig the ball out if it went there. The umpire kept signaling that the ball was in play, and the batter came all the way around for an inside-the-park homer.

"Sometimes," Hargrove said, "Manny does things that will baffle you. But he's not stupid. I see improvement every year."

Against Toronto, he moved in to field a looping single without accounting for the artificial turf. The ball bounced over his head and went to the wall; a single became a triple.

In Pittsburgh, he seemed to loaf after a single, which became a double, and allowed an extra run to score that lost the Indians the game. Another time this season, he trotted to first base on a ground out and Hargrove yanked him from the game.

Ramirez has a good arm, and his throws, noted David Justice, another Indians' outfielder, "are always right on the bag." And Justice, a good hitter in his own right, admires Ramirez's ability to connect on any pitch. "There's no pitch that Manny doesn't hit well," Justice said.

But it is on the basepaths that Ramirez has had his greatest problems. "He used to be very tentative," Hart said, "as though he didn't want to make a mistake that would embarrass him. He's still not a good base runner by any means, but he's working at it."

Gene Michael of the Yankees, scouting the Indians recently for the playoffs, said, "You have to balance the good with the bad with a player. And Manny does have some faults, but his hitting outweighs all the rest of them. I'd love to have him."

Ramirez came to the United States from the Dominican Republic, the son of a factory worker and a seamstress, when he was 12 years old. He signed as a first-round draft pick with the Indians in 1991, and still has a semester to go to graduate from high school. He is making $2 million a year and is signed through 1999 (the club has an option in 2000), when he will make $4 million, plus bonuses.

With the news media, he appears to have been influenced by two former teammates, Albert Belle and Eddie Murray, who were steadfast in their refusal to talk to reporters. Ramirez declined to be interviewed for this article; when asked recently to talk about his season, he said, "Just taking it easy, man, that's it," and walked away from his locker.

When Ramirez first came up to the major leagues, at age 21, Sparky Anderson, the Tigers' manager, said, "He's a baby who could develop into a monster."

Seems that Manny Ramirez, despite some very good days, is still developing.

ZIMMER:
UNLIKELY HERO OF '55 SERIES...
WELL, SORT OF

October 20, 2000

MAYBE YOU HEARD about how Popeye—he was simply called Don Zimmer in those days—was single-handedly responsible for the one and only time the Brooklyn Dodgers won the World Series, in 1955, in the first of back-to-back Subway Series with the Yankees. And he wasn't even playing. A lot of people aren't aware of how it happened, even fans in all the boroughs who have followed baseball right up to this weekend, when a Subway Series in these populous woods resumes after a parched 44-year interruption.

This time, of course, it's the Yankees against the Mets, inheritors of the hearts of many fans of the long-gone Dodgers and New York Giants. And Popeye will be the only man on either bench who was in uniform during the last two Subway Series. Zimmer, the bench coach to Yankee Manager Joe Torre, was a 24-year-old second baseman for the Dodgers in 1955.

He is called Popeye today at age 69 because he is puffy-cheeked, like the cartoon character. When you look at old photographs of Zimmer, say, turning the double play with Pee Wee Reese, he looks svelte—not quite Olive Oyl, but in the ballpark.

Since baseball thrives on history, as well as contemporary sound and fury, it is intriguing to learn how Popeye saw himself saving that long-ago day in '55. It was a sunlit October afternoon in Yankee

Stadium. Fans in the stands generally dressed more formally, with men in suits and fedoras and women in furs. Trolleys still ran in Brooklyn, and Eisenhower was planning to run for a second term.

The series was tied at three victories each when, in the top of the sixth, with the Dodgers ahead 2–0, Brooklyn manager Walter Alston, with lefty-righty switches, sent in George Shuba to pinch-hit for Zimmer against Bob Grim, who had been brought in to pitch that inning by Yankee manager Casey Stengel. Shuba grounded out. Now Junior Gilliam, the left fielder, moved to second base for Brooklyn, and Sandy Amoros went in to play left field.

In the bottom of the sixth, Billy Martin walked, Gil McDougald beat out a bunt, and Yogi Berra drove a certain extra-base hit to the left-field corner. But Amoros made a sensational catch and threw to Reese, who threw to Gil Hodges to double McDougald off first. Johnny Podres shut out the Yankees the rest of the way. "Remember," recalled Zimmer, sitting in the Yankee dugout before a team workout yesterday, "Amoros was left-handed and wore his glove on his right hand. A right-handed fielder cannot make that play in that corner. If I don't go out, Gilliam is still in the game. And we're in trouble with Yogi's hit. So, you see, with me on the bench, we won the game!"

He continued: "There was a team celebration in the Bossert Hotel in Brooklyn that night, and I'll never forget how happy the veterans especially were. Like Campy and Jackie and Erskine and Gil and Furillo and Newk. For years in the several other Subway Series, they could never beat the Yankees. The monkey was finally off their backs."

The next season, the Yankees and the Dodgers met again in a seven-game World Series, and the Yankees won. Zimmer sat on the bench, having suffered a fractured cheekbone after being hit by a pitch in June.

In 1958 the Dodgers and the Giants moved to California. Four years later the Mets surfaced. And who was the starting third baseman for this New York expansion team? Popeye. "The Mets lost 120 games that season," he said, "but you can only blame me for the first 20 or so. I was traded to Cincinnati 30 days into the season."

Eventually, Popeye managed the Red Sox. "The difference between those days and now?" he said. "I don't think there's the hatred between fans as there used to be, and not the hatred between the players either. The reason is that with free agency so many players move so much, it's hard to build up personal antagonisms. Like the Red Sox and Yankees of '76 and '77—there was Nettles against Lee, Fisk against Munson, Yaz and Piniella. And the old Dodgers and Yankees had the same players year after year. They weren't too thrilled with each other, either."

Despite the lack of animosity—a Clemens-versus-Piazza clash being relatively aberrant—he said, "This Subway Series is going to be unbelievable. It's been so long since there's been one, and these are two very good teams. Could go seven games. New York fans were waiting for this for the last two, three years, and it was close. I know the players are excited. The fever of the Subway Series is catching.

"Now," said Popeye, with his nearly half-century perspective, "now it's finally here, again."

VARITEK AND A-ROD BRAWL

September 16, 2004

WELL, YES, when Jason Varitek of the Boston Red Sox was stuffing his catcher's mitt into the matinee-idol profile of Yankee third baseman Alex Rodriguez—this being the baseball equivalent of a knuckle sandwich—they indeed had words. But exactly what were those words, and did they contain a classic insult to Rodriguez?

The incident, already elevated to the status of legend, occurred on July 24 in Boston in what became another chapter in the teams' ferocious rivalry for dominance of the American League East. It will surely be on the minds, as well as the tongues, of Yankee fans as the teams meet for three games this weekend in the Bronx, in the middle of another heated race.

In the third inning of that game, with Boston trailing 3–0, Bronson Arroyo hit Rodriguez with a pitch. Rodriguez jawed at Arroyo and was confronted by Varitek partway down the first-base line, and a scuffle ensued with both benches emptying. But the biggest blow came in the bottom of the ninth, when Bill Mueller hit a two-run homer off, of all people, closer Mariano Rivera, to give the Red Sox an 11–10 victory.

Varitek's altercation with Rodriguez is now viewed as one of those moments that turned Boston's season around, although it took the Red Sox a while to get going. Three weeks after the incident, they trailed the Yankees by 10½ games, and it was only then that they went on a tear that wiped away most of the Yankees' lead and confirmed their status as George Steinbrenner's biggest headache.

One question remains, however: did Varitek, as rumor has it, spit out a Bartlett's-style insult at Rodriguez? Did he say, "We don't throw at .260 hitters"?

"That's ridiculous," said Varitek, sitting at his locker before a recent game. "I'm not that smart to come up with such a clever line in the heat of battle. I knew Arroyo didn't hit him on purpose, and I just told him to get along to first base."

Perhaps he did not say exactly that—Varitek and Rodriguez, who has since lifted his average to .290, were both suspended for four games for their activities—but "not that smart" is a statement that will find argument among the Red Sox themselves.

For Varitek is considered "the unquestioned team leader," as the pitching coach, Dave Wallace, termed it, and "a big part of the heart and soul of the club," in the words of Theo Epstein, the team's general manager.

And pitcher Curt Schilling, who leads the majors with 19 victories in his first season with the Red Sox, said of Varitek, "He studies the opposing hitters to such a degree, and fits this knowledge with the particular abilities of the pitchers, that his signal-calling is amazing. It seems that every time I shake him off, something bad happens."

Boston manager Terry Francona added, paraphrasing a line from an old television commercial, "When Jason speaks, people listen."

Varitek said he understood that he will be the primary target of invective in Yankee Stadium on Friday night, taking over a role previously assumed by Red Sox pitcher Pedro Martínez, who, in a bench-clearing tussle during a playoff game last season at Fenway, tossed Don Zimmer, then a 72-year-old Yankee coach, to the ground.

And Varitek, being as thick of body—6′2″, 230 pounds—as he is nimble of mind, will be a big target, too.

He is 32, in his seventh season with the Red Sox, the only major league team he has played for, and no stranger to Yankee Stadium and the Beantown-Gotham conflict.

"I've gotten booed there before," Varitek said. "It's expected. We're the villains in their eyes. And because of that one incident, me especially. But Alex and I were about the same thing. We're on opposing teams, and we're trying to win."

Varitek was an All-American at Georgia Tech, *Baseball America*'s college player of the year in 1993, a first-round draft pick by the Seattle Mariners in 1994 and destined for big things in Boston after the Red Sox acquired him and Derek Lowe in 1997 for reliever Heathcliff Slocumb. He can hit from either side of the plate, rare for a catcher, and last season, his first as an All-Star, he batted .273 with 25 home runs and 85 runs batted in.

This season, he has been just as formidable with a bat, batting .304 with 17 home runs and 66 RBIs. He bats just below the middle of the imposing Red Sox lineup and has been one of the hottest hitters in the American League since the All-Star break.

But, noted Epstein, "His offense comes second in his mind to his work behind the plate and with the pitchers."

"He takes responsibility for their performance," Epstein said. "This attitude of team and winning rubs off on his teammates."

And if the Red Sox finally vanquish the Yankees in the regular season and go to the World Series in October—they have finished second to the Yankees in six straight seasons, a major league record—Varitek will be given credit for being, as Dan Shaughnessy of the *Boston Globe* wrote, "the de facto captain of the team."

Varitek said the Red Sox were good last year, but not quite as good as the Yankees, even though the Red Sox were leading the Yankees by three runs with five outs to go in Game 7 of the American League Championship Series. That was the game in which the Yankees rallied off Martínez in the eighth to tie the score and won it in the eleventh on a home run by Aaron Boone, with Varitek behind the plate as the Red Sox failed again.

"We didn't beat ourselves," Varitek said. "They beat us. Have to give them credit. When we look back, what happened last season didn't discourage or depress us. In fact, it has given us confidence. The feeling in this clubhouse is, if we just play the way we're capable of, then this year is our year."

A notion that, this weekend, will be tested in the Bronx.

[The Red Sox went on to beat the Yankees in the ALCS 4–3 and swept the St. Louis Cardinals 4–0 in the World Series.]

A-ROD IN JAPANESE TRANSLATION

July 24, 2006

WHEN HE WAS SIGNED by the Seattle Mariners to a three-year contract for $16.5 million before this season, the concern about Kenji Johjima was whether he could communicate with the pitchers as the first Japanese catcher in the major leagues.

Now, several months into his first major league season, and with Johjima having taken crash courses in English, the jury is in.

When Joe—as he is called by his teammates, who have an easier time with that than with his given name—goes to the mound to talk, George Sherrill, a left-handed relief pitcher, was asked, can he communicate?

"Sort of," he said in the visitors' clubhouse last week before the Mariners played an afternoon game in the Bronx against the Yankees.

What does "sort of" mean?

"Well, the English is broken, but, really, it's easily understandable," Sherrill said. "You know, baseball is a universal language. Joe knows enough to say something like 'your shoulder is flying open too quick,' and so I tighten my delivery a little. But I think I only shook him off twice all year. He's done a tremendous job."

What has it been like for J.J. Putz, the Seattle closer, to communicate with Johjima?

"It's like ordering sushi," he said, with a smile. "You have a certain amount of words in common, and you do a certain amount of pointing."

And when that does not work, said Ron Hassey, the catching coach, "we've got the Japanese interpreter in the runway off the dugout."

"But that's rare," Hassey added. "All of us understand 'throw the breaking ball here,' or 'fastball inside.'"

The 30-year-old Johjima, who was an all-star in Japan the previous six seasons, has done well enough that after yesterday's game, he has caught more innings, 720, than any other catcher in the major leagues.

He is hitting .286 with 10 homers and 43 runs batted in, and he is ninth among major league catchers with 28 extra-base hits....

Over the recent All-Star break, Johjima flew home to see his newborn baby.

And what, he was asked, will the boy be when he grows up?

"A writer," he said, immediately establishing his credentials in public relations.

Johjima not only speaks to his teammates, but he will also sometimes talk to an opponent. An example of this occurred in a Yankees game last week.

When Alex Rodriguez went to the plate, Johjima greeted him with "Hello," then added something else in English.

"I didn't quite get what he was saying," Rodriguez said. "And then he pointed. I thought he was messing with me. So I looked over to Jerry Meals."

Meals was the home-plate umpire.

"Jerry told me, 'He says your fly is open,'" Rodriguez said.

And it was. The zipper was broken. As soon as he could, Rodriguez changed his pants.

Johjima shrugged when the incident was related to him.

"I was just trying to be helpful," he said. "I asked him if that was part of his batting routine. And we both laughed."

TED WILLIAMS:
AN EVENING WITH THE KID

November 12, 1988

BOSTON, MASSACHUSETTS — He was once called "the Kid." He also had other nicknames: the Splendid Splinter, the Thumper, Teddy Ballgame. None of them quite apply anymore for Ted Williams, who recently turned 70 years old, except the Kid.

No longer is he a splinter, splendid or otherwise, and he thumps no baseballs as in days of yore, nor plays any ballgames, and hasn't for nearly 30 years.

But there is still the en-thoos-iasm, as he says the word, the stubbornness, perhaps, the dream of striving to be the best and striving for the best that marked him as a boy, surely, and as a young man, certainly, and as a senior citizen, absolutely.

On Thursday night in the Wang Center here, Theodore Samuel Williams, the last of the .400 hitters, the Kid, returned for kids. It was a benefit in his honor, "An Evening with 9, and Friends," for the Jimmy Fund, a fund-raising arm of the Dana-Farber Cancer Institute, with a special interest in children's cancer.

For 40 years Williams, who, no Red Sox fan need be told, wore the red No. 9 of their team, has been closely associated with the Jimmy Fund. He has visited ailing children, usually without photographers, attended affairs for the fund, and always lent his name to the cause. Never, though, until now, would he consent to be honored at a fund-raiser.

"It took an awful, awful, awful awful lot to get me here," he said before the evening's program. "I just thought there were millions and millions of people who've done a lot more for this than I have."

Friends finally prevailed, and Williams arrived even wearing a tie; he rarely submits to such a silly social convention. It was a black string tie held at the neck by a silver oval clasp with an embossed gold salmon, for, as the world knows, Williams is as avid about catching a fish as he was about clubbing a baseball.

For the evening with Williams, 4,200 people filled the ornate old theater and paid a total of $250,000 that went to the Jimmy Fund.

The friends of Williams, introduced one by one and "interviewed" by David Hartman on a stage set like a fishing cabin, included former teammates like Dom DiMaggio and Bobby Doerr, rivals like Joe DiMaggio and Bob Feller; Tommy Lasorda and Reggie Jackson; John Glenn, who was Williams' squadron commander as a fighter pilot in the war in Korea; Tip O'Neill, the former Speaker of the House from Boston; Bud Leavitt, a Maine sportswriter and longtime fishing pal of Williams; and Stephen King, the writer and a New Englander, who represented baseball fandom and Williams fandom.

King spoke of our greatest baseball heroes as having "a resonance that others don't have," such as rock stars or movie stars. Their careers become the stuff of legends. And Williams perhaps resonated more than most, not only because of his extraordinary baseball prowess, but because of his dedication and his humanity, even his vulnerability: he might be quick to anger, would hold a grudge, he stubbornly refused to hit to left when teams packed the right side of the field in the notorious "Williams shift."

And there was in Williams that core of boyish delight in playing the game. When he first came up to the Red Sox in the spring of 1939, he informed the veterans with callow forthrightness about left field: "Hey, this job is mine!"

He cared so much about doing so well. Doerr recalled that Williams, the perfectionist, once stepped out of the batter's box and waited for a cloud to go by because the shadow it created was distracting to him. A film clip at one point showed Williams hitting a homer and nearly galloping with glee around the bases. The audience laughed with appreciation.

Lasorda came out and said, "He was electrifying with a bat in his hands, like a beautiful painting. Enough about Joe DiMaggio." More laughs.

But both Williams and DiMaggio were electrifying at the plate.

"Dom, who was the best hitter you ever saw?" asked Hartman, of the bespectacled DiMaggio known as the Little Professor.

The audience hushed. "Well," said Dom DiMaggio, "the best right-handed hitter"—the audience roared at the unexpected but perfect cop-out—"was Joe. But the best left-handed hitter by far was Ted Williams."

Feller recalled how he could never get his famous fastball by Williams. Joe DiMaggio, his hair now all white, spoke of his admiration for "the best hitter I ever saw." And Reggie Jackson told of the encouragement Williams gave him as a rookie: "Never let anybody change your swing." Jackson called him "a real nice American natural resource."

Williams' son, John Henry, a young man, brought out a five-year-old boy named Joey Raymundo, who was wearing a tuxedo. Joey has leukemia and is being treated at the clinic. He presented Williams with a gift from the fund, an oil painting—the frame was as big as the boy—of Williams in baseball action.

Then Williams sat down and pulled out some notes—along with a pair of glasses. "Not a lot of people have seen these," said the man who was known for having remarkable eyesight.

He spoke of how lucky his life had been, and, to a question from Hartman, said, "You're not gonna make this old guy cry."

Finally, Williams looked around at his friends seated nearby on the stage and out to the audience.

"This has been an honor," he said, "and I'm thrilled and a little embarrassed." He paused. "And I wanna thank you."

And despite his resistance, there was a slight catch in his throat and, it seemed, a little moisture in the Kid's eye.

ABOUT THE AUTHOR

IRA BERKOW, a sports columnist and feature writer for the *New York Times* for more than 25 years, shared the Pulitzer Prize for national reporting in 2001 and was a finalist for the Pulitzer for commentary in 1988. He also was a reporter for the *Minneapolis Tribune* and a columnist for Newspaper Enterprise Association. He is the author of 19 books, including the bestsellers *Red: A Biography of Red Smith* and *Maxwell Street: Survival in a Bazaar*, and, most recently, the author of *The Corporal Was a Pitcher: The Courage of Lou Brissie*. His work has frequently been cited in the prestigious anthology series, *Best American Sports Writing*, as well as the 1999 anthology *Best American Sports Writing of the Century*. He holds a bachelor's degree from Miami University (Ohio) and a master's degree from Northwestern University's Medill School of Journalism, and has been honored with distinguished professional achievement awards from both schools. In 2009 he was inducted into the International Jewish Sports Hall of Fame and also received an Honorary Doctorate of Humane Letters from Roosevelt University in Chicago. Mr. Berkow lives in New York City.